Extreme Programming
Pocket Guide

Extreme Programming
Pocket Guide

chromatic

Beijing · Cambridge · Farnham · Köln · Paris · Sebastopol · Taipei · Tokyo

Extreme Programming Pocket Guide

by chromatic

Copyright © 2003 O'Reilly Media, Inc. All rights reserved.
Printed in the United States of America.

Published by O'Reilly Media, Inc., 1005 Gravenstein Highway North, Sebastopol, CA 95472.

O'Reilly Media, Inc. books may be purchased for educational, business, or sales promotional use. Online editions are also available for most titles (*safari.oreilly.com*). For more information, contact our corporate/institutional sales department: (800) 998-9938 or *corporate@oreilly.com*.

Editor:	Tatiana Apandi Diaz
Production Editor:	Genevieve d'Entremont
Cover Designer:	Emma Colby
Interior Designer:	David Futato

Printing History:

July 2003:   First Edition.

0-596-00485-0
[C]   [5/04]

Contents

Part III. XP Events

Part IV. Extreme Programming Artifacts

Part V. Roles in Extreme Programming

Foreword

This is the most important Extreme Programming book written to date. It is the most complete and concise overview of the words all Extreme Programmers use to describe what they do. Until now, those wishing to understand Extreme Programming had to piece together the lore of the movement from innovative but now overly voluminous sources. The community has grown to where it needs this book.

Extreme Programming's roots started with a few people on a few projects taking a fresh look at what they do. It could have been any number of such small groups—the ideas of Extreme Programming have been invented over and over. But one group took advantage of the unique properties of the World Wide Web to articulate, refine, and expand their ideas in an ever enlarging community.

My own web site, the Portland Pattern Repository's Wiki-WikiWeb, gave voice to this community at its founding. Wiki lets readers become writers and trusts them to organize their writing to meet their own needs. The result is a collection of terms that have very precise and universally accepted meanings, even though they may not appear so at first glance.

That is why we need this book now. Our movement is blessed with a wonderful series of books that explains the counterintuitive logic of the methods from every perspective. These books served the second generation of Extreme Programmers who were willing to buck the prevailing wisdom in order to get to a better place. But now Extreme Programming is becoming the prevailing wisdom, and not every convert wants to (or has time to) relive its founding. We're going to need stacks of this book.

This is the guide for you, the third generation of Extreme Programmers. You probably chose Extreme Programming based on its reputation. You don't need to be convinced, but you do need to understand. Be you sponsor, manager, customer, tester, user, or developer, if you are involved in an Extreme Programming project, then you are an Extreme Programmer. Welcome to the team. Here is your handbook. Now let's get to work.

—Ward Cunningham
Cunningham & Cunningham, Inc.

Preface

There's a word for software that cannot be changed after delivery. That word is hardware.

In the early days of computer programming, processor time was expensive. If you had an error that kept your program from running, it could be days or weeks before you had the chance to try again. Any change could ripple through the rest of your program. To save time and money, you'd have to be completely sure your program would work before it reached the computer. You could spend hours poring over your code.

The obvious lesson was *change is painful and expensive*.

A few decades later, *Extreme Programming* (hereafter called *XP*) claims otherwise. It's possible to develop high-quality software despite—or even because of—change. XP's great assumption is that a little bit of planning, a little bit of coding, and a little bit of testing let you decide if you're right or wrong while it's still cheap to change your mind. You still need some idea where you're going, but you don't have to commit to an exact itinerary. You can change your mind along the way without spending a fortune.

XP is a software development method that emphasizes simplicity, feedback, courage, and communication. It's partly a reaction to the pervasive belief that change is bad and avoidable. Kent Beck introduced XP in *Extreme Programming Explained* (Addison-Wesley) as a collection of 12 fundamental XP practices. Few of these practices are new—they've been part of the canon of best practices for decades. What *is* unique to XP is how they build on and reinforce each other.

In the past few years, thousands of programmers and companies have discovered that XP helps them produce better, more reliable software with less stress. XP concepts have even infiltrated vocabularies and toolsets outside of XP teams. Consider, for example, the renewed interest in testing and testing tools among software engineers.

Effective software development is difficult, no matter what your method. Being able to adapt to change at a moment's notice requires tremendous discipline and care. The strength of your team—your good habits and best practices—are vital to the success of your project.

There are many ways to write good software. Straight, by-the-book XP is one of those ways. A well-disciplined, extremely smart, and highly motivated team can probably produce the right software that does the right thing at the right price with any reasonable development process. The rest of us need something more.

Any reasonable process has its strengths and weaknesses. Many software development teams pick and choose practices from many approaches. XP has an edge because its 12 core practices reinforce and draw upon each other. The strengths of one practice fill in for the weaknesses of another. Understanding XP's values and practices and their relationships will help you adopt it successfully. You must play to its strengths and avoid its pitfalls. (Thankfully, if you're doing XP as a whole, its pitfalls are few.)

XP is ideal for a small group of developers within a company, writing software for that company. It's easy to find a real customer. The software can be delivered frequently. The outcome isn't obvious from the start; change is normal.

XP tends to add little value to projects that know exactly what they must build. Why optimize for change if it rarely happens? Of course, several XP practices can help any software project.

This book explores XP and its parts. It's arranged topically, exploring the assumptions, practices, artifacts, events, roles, and guidelines individually. Each section stands alone as much as possible. Though XP was carefully crafted to fit together as a whole, exploring each idea on its own allows this book to serve as a reference in the heat of a project.

This book is aimed primarily at developers. Many development methods treat programmers almost as interchangeable cogs in a machine. XP is different, partly because it evolves with the experiences of practicing programmers, and partly because it strips away so much nonessential work. Of course, XP also puts developers and customers in close proximity, so sections of the book apply to customers, too.

Ideally, you will be able to adopt XP completely on your project. Practically, changing your team and your organization will take time. You may decide to adopt XP in stages or adopt only a few practices. XP may be too extreme for you to adopt right now, but understanding how it fits together can help you improve an existing process or create a new process.

The goal of software development is to create good systems that meet business needs with the available resources. XP can help you do just that.

Overview of This Book

This book contains eight sections, arranged topically:

Part I, *Why XP?*
   Describes XP, the problem it's intended to solve, and its values

Part II, *Extreme Programming Practices*
   Explains the 12 core practices of XP

Part III, *XP Events*
    Details the events of an XP project

Part IV, *Extreme Programming Artifacts*
    Excavates XP's physical artifacts

Part V, *Roles in Extreme Programming*
    Introduces the major and minor roles people play in XP

Part VI, *Coding, XP Style*
    Defines XP's coding principles

Part VII, *Adopting XP*
    Suggests a plan by which you can adopt XP

Part VIII, *Further Resources*
    Lists further resources

Typographic Conventions

This book uses the following typographic conventions:

Italic
    Used for new terms where they are defined and for emphasis

`Constant width`
    Used for class names and any literal text

Comments and Questions

Please address comments and questions concerning this book to the publisher:

O'Reilly & Associates, Inc.
1005 Gravenstein Highway North
Sebastopol, CA 95472
(800) 998-9938 (in the United States or Canada)
(707) 829-0515 (international/local)
(707) 829-0104 (fax)

There is a web page for this book, which lists errata, examples, or any additional information. You can access this page at:

http://www.oreilly.com/catalog/extprogpg/

To comment or ask technical questions about this book, send email to:

bookquestions@oreilly.com

For more information about books, conferences, Resource Centers, and the O'Reilly Network, see the O'Reilly web site at:

http://www.oreilly.com/

Acknowledgments

To start, I'd like to thank Tim O'Reilly for proposing this idea and my editors, Linda Mui and Tatiana Diaz, for helping to make it a reality.

The size of this book belies the hard work of many friends and colleagues who provided reviews and advice. In alphabetical order, they are Kate Agena, Ann Barcomb, Tony Bowden, Sarah Breen, Ward Cunningham, Schuyler Erle, Nick Forrette, Jim Little, Rob Nagler, Aleatha Parker, Karen Pauley, Curtis Poe, Allison Randal, and Dave Thomas. With people this smart, any remaining errors and omissions are obviously mine alone.

This book is dedicated to my nephew, Jacob Edward, whose release date somehow preceded mine. I'm trying to make the world better for you, buddy.

PART I

Why XP?

*[The] cost of fixing things increases profoundly
the longer we wait.*

*Stretching out design just makes the errors cost /more/,
whether found inside design or in a later phase.*

*The right lesson is [to] find out right away whether we've made
a mistake. The best way to do that is to take an idea through
analysis, design, code, and test in the shortest possible time.*

—Ron Jeffries[*]

Many software development methods assert that change is
expensive. A bug caught in the maintenance phase of a
project tends to cost more than a bug caught in the planning
phase, as shown in Figure 1. Extreme Programming makes a
different claim: *it's possible to keep the cost of changing software from rising dramatically with time.*

What kind of software would you develop if you had the
freedom to adapt to changing requirements and environ-
ments with grace and ease? Given sufficient time and
resources, what could you accomplish? Is your goal even
realistic? If so, how can you achieve it? XP attempts to
answer all of these questions.

---

[*] 8 July 2002, on the XP Mailing List (*http://groups.yahoo.com/group/
extremeprogramming/message/55241*).

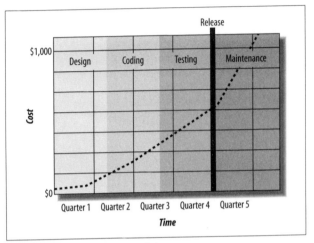

Figure 1. The traditional cost-of-change curve

Who Cares About Process, Anyway?

Talking about customer rights and business changes may not matter much to you. *Methodology*—discussing methods of developing software—may seem dull and impractical. Does it really matter?

A project's development method sets its values and guidelines. If your project values lots of written documentation, you'll produce it. If your project values reliability, you'll spend time on testing and proving code correctness.

Of course, what people actually do also affects your project's culture. No matter how well-intentioned your values, if your methods aren't practiced, they're useless. A method that recommends voluminous design documents is just creating busywork if no one ever reads the documents, let alone updates them.

The development method you actually practice determines the kind of team you have and the kind of software you produce. You may tell prospective developers that everyone works a forty-hour week, but you can't really guarantee that unless you know how to avoid the death march before a release. You might tell the customer that all code is reviewed, but unless developers actually check each other's code, what good is saying the code has been reviewed?

The only way to save a troubled project or a troubled team is to figure out what's broken and then fix it. Every development method is designed to solve some problem. Changing your project or your team is possible, with time. Following a good development method is a great place to start.

This book discusses XP's values, how it goes about achieving those goals, and how to adopt those goals on your own project. First, you have to understand how XP views software development.

The XP Equation

Software projects can be managed in terms of four variables: *time*, *scope*, *resources*, and *quality*. Every project works under some combination of these variables. Even if they're not measured directly, their interactions shape your project.

Imagine a water filtration plant on a space station, as shown in Figure 2. A reservoir of unpotable water sits on one side of the plant, and potable water flows to the station inhabitants from the other side. In this closed system, water re-enters the reservoir very quickly.* The plant has a control panel with four dials, labeled Time, Resources, Scope, and Quality. Each dial controls an aspect of the filtration process.

---

* This demonstrates the XP principle of a metaphoric vocabulary. See "Coding Practice 4: Develop a Common Vocabulary" in Part II for how this vocabulary helps to communicate larger ideas.

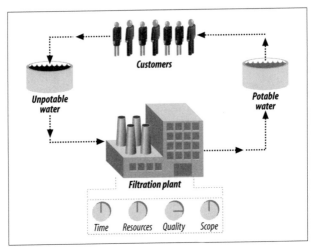

Figure 2. A closed water cycle

This image can also represent software development, as shown in Figure 3. A customer makes a request; this unfinished work, or business problem, is the unpotable water supply. The request is implemented by developers; this is the filtration process. The finished request is delivered to the customer in the form of a code solution; this is the potable water. Based on the results, the customer makes another request and the cycle continues. The water represents the software itself, continually being refined in a tight loop.

The Time dial adjusts the amount of time spent filtering water. This is a limiting factor. If the other dials remain constant, running the plant for a week will produce a greater amount of potable water than running the plant for a day.

The Resources dial changes the amount of equipment that will be used to filter water. This is also a limiting factor, taking into account maintenance workers, overseers, electricity, and everything else that keeps the plant in operation. If the other dials remain constant, running the plant with ten filters will produce more potable water than running the plant

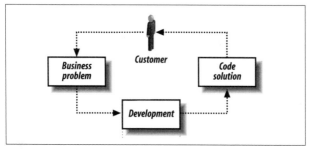

Figure 3. An XP cycle

with one. It's possible to have an overabundance of resources; for example, having more employees than available work. In this case, productivity will plateau despite the additional resources. If the extra resources themselves need supporting resources, such as additional supervisors for excess employees, productivity may even decrease.

The Scope dial adjusts the amount of potable water the plant will produce. This is an enabling factor. Suppose the plant normally produces a thousand gallons of potable water in a day. If half of the filters are offline, the scope must be reduced to fifty percent of capacity unless time is increased or quality is decreased. If scope is increased, time or resources must increase or quality must decrease.

The Quality dial is more complex. Few projects ever decrease quality directly. Increasing scope without increasing time or resources or reducing time or resources without decreasing scope tends to decrease quality indirectly. Increased pressures on time or resources eventually force quality downward as well. If there are fewer people to maintain the plant or if filters run longer between maintenance and cleaning, quality suffers. Increasing quality can decrease pressure on time or resources. Assuming the water system is closed and the station residents produce a constant amount of pollution, the cleaner the water the plant produces, the less filtering it will need in the next cycle.

Quality should generally remain fixed. Different projects will have different quality needs, however, and those needs may change over time. A station that has lost its reserves from an asteroid strike might prefer less filtered water that can be delivered more quickly.

Many projects concentrate on time and resources, assuming that quality will stay fixed. If scope *ever* changes, it's usually increased (e.g., when customers ask for new features). Worse, time and resources are often reduced or, at best, kept constant. Release dates are brought forward and developers are removed from the project. The only remaining adjustment point—quality—slips downward.

XP suggests a different strategy. Agree as a team—including the customer—on an acceptable level of quality. Agree to consider that time and resources are fixed. The only remaining question is that of scope. What will be delivered? When will it be delivered? The customer will set priorities for individual features. You will work on them in turn. The software will always be kept in a releasable state.

XP recommends adjusting scope regularly, even daily. Every business decision may affect the project. XP takes advantage of this by making changes and their effects visible to the people responsible for making business decisions. If the water is cleaner than normal, scope can increase. If the plant must close early for a holiday, scope should decrease. By monitoring the four variables closely, software can be planned, developed, and delivered more deliberately and predictably.

Given healthy communication within the team, rapid feedback on the state of the project, and the ability to adjust scope as necessary, XP practitioners are free to assume sufficient resources. This is the other fundamental assumption of Extreme Programming: *exposing the tradeoffs of changes leads to fewer surprises and smoother development*. You may even grow to enjoy change.

XP Values

XP has four main values: communication, feedback, simplicity, and courage. All of XP's practices support these values.

Communication

Good communication is essential to any project. Honest, regular communication allows you to adjust to change. This is how developers know what to do and how the customer knows when it will be done. Hiding or ignoring information can sink your project.

XP asks people in business roles to make business decisions and people in technical roles to make technical decisions. Customers answer the questions "What will be done?" and "What are the priorities?" Developers answer the questions "How will this be accomplished?" and "How long will each step take?" Developers trust the business people to identify features and their priorities, because they know the problem domain. Business people trust the developers to identify and to estimate the work that must be done, because they know the technology. Each group takes responsibility for its own decisions. Both groups are part of the same team, devoted to meeting the customer's needs.

XP puts developers and customers in constant communication. A customer works with you to set business priorities and to answer questions. The customer must analyze the project both as a real user and from a business point of view. The customer sees the team's progress every day and can adjust the work schedule as needed. The customer works with developers to produce tests to verify that a feature is present and works as expected. When you have a question about a feature, ask the customer directly. A five-minute, face-to-face conversation peppered with body language, gestures, and whiteboard drawings communicates more than an email exchange or a conference call can.

Removing the communication barriers between customers and developers increases your flexibility. Sharpening the distinction between business and technical decisions helps you make the right decisions. Communicating clearly about goals, status, and priorities allows you to succeed.

Feedback

Feedback means asking questions and learning from the answers. The only way to know what a customer really wants is to ask him. The only way to know if the code does what it really should do is to test it. The sooner you can get feedback, the more time you have to react to it.

XP provides rapid, frequent feedback. Every XP practice is part of a built-in feedback loop. The best way to flatten the cost-of-change curve is to listen to and learn from all of these sources as often as possible. This is why XP concentrates on frequent planning, designing, testing, and communicating. Some changes may still be expensive, but they tend to be cheaper when practiced in short cycles with rapid feedback (see Figure 4).

Rapid feedback reduces the investment of time and resources in ideas with little payoff. Failures are found as soon as possible, within days or weeks rather than months or years. Though planning ahead can avoid some mistakes, it's only through actual work that you can understand your real obstacles. This feedback helps you to refine your schedule and your plans. It allows you to steer your project back on track as soon as someone notices a problem. It identifies when a feature is finished and when it will cost more or less than previously believed. It builds confidence that the system does just what the customer really wants.

Frequent feedback allows you to make frequent adjustments and to learn from them. The shorter the time between making an estimate and actually implementing a feature, the easier it is for you to review your estimate. Learning from this review process will make your future estimates more accurate. For the

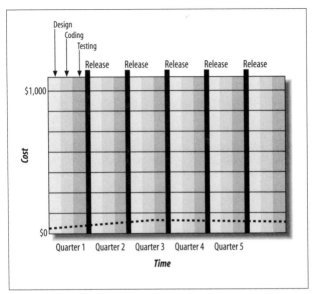

Figure 4. XP's cost-of-change curve

customer, seeing a feature implemented leads to a better understanding of the software and how it works. If he can review the feature as it's implemented, he can make suggestions that can be implemented rapidly. Thus, the period between design and implementation is measured in hours and minutes. Mistakes can be noticed and corrected before they ossify.

Feedback from testing helps you to be confident about making changes. Whether adding a new feature or improving the design of the code, knowing that a change in the last 10 minutes (or even 10 seconds) has broken a test reduces the amount of debugging detective work to manageable chunks.

The feedback from frequent releases gives the customer confidence in the value of the project. His investment begins to pay off quickly. He sees his most important features implemented as soon as possible. Regular and reliable successes demonstrate the benefits of XP.

Simplicity

Simplicity means building only the system that really needs to be built. It means solving only today's problems today. Complexity costs a lot and predicting the future is hard. You have to wait for the future to see if you were right.

Armed with communication and feedback, it's much easier to know exactly what you need. You don't have to guess. You can just ask. If you practice simplicity, it should be as easy to add a feature when it becomes necessary as it would be to add it today.

Courage

Courage means making the hard decisions when necessary. If a feature isn't working, fix it. If some code isn't up to snuff, improve it. If you're not going to deliver everything you promised on schedule, tell the customer. Decide what you can deliver and do it.

Courage is a difficult virtue to apply. No one wants to be wrong or to break a promise. The only way to recover from a mistake, though, is to admit to it and to fix it. Delivering software is challenging, but meeting that challenge instead of avoiding it leads to better software.

Assuming Sufficiency

Software development is often a competition for time and resources: managers fight developers, developers fight managers, and everyone fights customers.

XP asks a different question. Given sufficient time and resources, how would you develop software?

Sufficient Time

XP enables sufficient development time. Rather than scrambling to meet an impossible deadline, work at your normal pace. The amount of work you can do is constant—the only real question is which work to do. Adjust scope to fit the schedule to the available time.

"Sufficient time" also implies that change is inexpensive—that the customer can change his priorities cheaply and you can change the code easily. Several XP practices combine to produce flexible code.

XP attempts to produce the most valuable software for the time and resources invested. To do this, you must be able to estimate accurately the amount of work you can actually do. The customer must be able to identify the most important work that can be done. You must be able to change both the schedule and the software as the customer's needs change. Of course, it may be impossible to fit the desired work into the schedule. XP attempts to identify this as soon as possible so that the customer can stop the project before he invests too heavily without payoff.

XP projects work in very short cycles, reducing the length of time between an action and its analysis. There are many opportunities to judge the current progress and to make course corrections. The project starts producing results almost immediately. You can see if you're on the right track very soon. You'll have plenty of time if you make the most of the time you have.

Sufficient Resources

XP enables sufficient development resources. The number of developers governs the amount of work you can do. Adjust scope to fit the project to the available resources.

Developers provide estimates for very small tasks. Refine your estimates by comparing them to the actual time spent on the tasks. With a little experience, your estimates will be good enough for planning purposes. Your estimates give the customer a resource budget that he can spend on scheduling features.

Resources tend to increase with time, in the sense that you'll gain more experience with the project. You'll learn more about the problem you're solving, develop new techniques, and refine your skills. As the code evolves, it will be easier to add new features—especially as you solve the customer's most pressing needs.

Constant Cost of Change

XP ensures that the cost of change remains constant over time. In other words, it will cost about as much to add a feature next year as it would to add that feature today. If this is true, you can defer features until they're really necessary, without worrying about the cost of waiting. XP invests time and resources where they will produce the most results.

XP reduces the cost of change by seeking out continual customer feedback. The customer will receive a working version of the code as soon as possible, often just a few weeks after the start of the project. Development then becomes a process of refinement. Regular, frequent releases add new features and improve existing features. The customer watches his requests take shape. Business changes are reflected in code and delivered to end users with surprising speed.

The development cycle provides regular, frequent opportunities for the customer to adjust the schedule to match business needs. He can change the project's priorities at any point. He can even stop the project when he's recouped his investment. At the same time, developers are constantly refining their understanding of the software and the business problem.

XP produces flexible and maintainable code by emphasizing simplicity and verification. Rigorous testing gives everyone confidence that the code meets customer requirements. Individual pieces work well together. Future changes won't mysteriously break the existing, correct behavior. Developers can improve the code with small, measured changes, and are free to address new requirements fearlessly.

Developer Effectiveness

Good software requires good developers. Effective development requires programmers of ability, broad knowledge, and productivity. XP takes advantage of the best practices of programming, introducing and reinforcing good developer habits. A group of average developers who are dedicated and committed to producing good software can become a highly productive team.

XP's practices form a network of checks and balances. For example, developers work in pairs. Two sets of eyes review every line of code. Two brains evaluate each solution. Ideas flow freely—they're analyzed and are implemented if they make the project simpler, more correct, or more maintainable.

XP sets up several feedback loops in the coding process. Disciplined tests provide immediate results and probe the project's health. Estimates are soon explored, leading to better accuracy. The entire codebase—design and implementation—is open for improvement when it's needed. Expect your project to evolve into its optimal form. Watch change happen and learn from your mistakes. This will quickly build valuable experience.

XP removes several barriers that hamper effective development. By trusting the technical decisions of developers and the business decisions of customers, XP limits the responsibilities of each group. By agreeing to adjust the scope dial while leaving time alone, XP avoids overwork and frustration that sap morale and reduce efficacy. By valuing honesty, improving communication, and working more closely as a team, XP will help you succeed—as a team.

Freedom to Experiment

XP assumes that the entire team—managers, developers, and customers—has the freedom to experiment. This affects every decision, big and small. XP can flourish only in a culture where it is acceptable to ask "Is there a better way to do this?" and "What can we stop doing and still succeed?" There is no reward without risk.

XP assumes that teams have the freedom to remove obstacles. For example, many teams prefer to work in large, open areas. It may be difficult to escape cubicles, but removing physical barriers to collaboration can improve productivity dramatically. If you can overcome this problem and demonstrate that the change had a positive effect, you may find it easier to remove further obstacles.

XP attempts to reduce risk without waiting for perfect solutions. If good enough is good enough, why wait? Aim in the right direction and make course corrections as you go. Projects require a small, up-front investment of time and resources. They will begin to deliver usable results within a few weeks. The customer can immediately make adjustments toward a better solution, or even end the project if necessary.

XP reserves the right for teams to change their culture. Keep in mind the goal: to produce effective software by doing what's really important. XP sets guidelines to determine what's important, but it's up to you to apply them to your team.

PART II

Extreme Programming Practices

XP's 12 practices rely on and support each other. Their feedback helps guide your decisions. Their interactions help you to achieve high levels of productivity and quality. It's possible to write good software with only a few practices, but XP works best with every piece in play—the whole is much greater than the sum of its parts.

Each practice can have several roles. For example, testing influences design and encourages small, controlled experiments. It also applies conservative pressure for stability. Picking and choosing a few practices without appreciating how they support each other can lead to dramatic failures—refactoring without a rigorous test suite can introduce subtle bugs that need extensive debugging. Although this chapter attempts to explain the ideas behind each practice and how it fits into XP as a whole, the best way to understand XP is to practice it in its entirety.

Doing XP by the book requires discipline. While a team of the world's very best developers might practice test-driven development fully, the rest of us need the positive peer pressure of a programming partner to resist the temptation to put off testing. Though many of the practices can improve your software on their own, they're less effective when removed from their supporting framework.

If XP as a whole is truly impossible and not merely impractical for you, be cautious about adopting XP piecemeal. With the right team, you can find a combination of natural talent and discipline that allows you to get by with a subset of XP, though you will face additional challenges. You can still see great benefits, but you will take on more risk. There are many ways to develop great software. XP is one way, but other development methods fit different circumstances and solve different needs.

This chapter divides the XP practices into three groups: the practice of coding, the interaction between developers as you produce code, and the relationship between business and technical interests.

Coding Practices

Writing code is the most important practice in software development—very few projects can succeed without writing code.* Most of the time and energy devoted to a project are concentrated on producing code. Consequently, XP is very much concerned with code.

The code is the most important artifact of the project—without it, the project does nothing. It is the final authority on how the system actually behaves. As a developer, code is your business. This focus worries many people, who fear that XP is the domain of cowboy coders who jump headfirst into hacking without planning. This is not the case. XP uses working code to validate and to evaluate its plans. The four coding practices work together to produce code that is easy to maintain and extend and is always ready to be delivered to the customer.

Coding Practice 1: Code and Design Simply

Goal: to produce software that's easy to change.

Code and design simply. Solve the customer's current need. Resist the urge to guess at future needs, whether you're

---

* It's possible that the right decision is not to do a project after analyzing its risks and requirements. This should also be counted as a success. Other success markers include acceptable quality levels and the quality of life of developers, managers, and customers.

designing the next feature or coding it. XP has three rules that govern simplicity: Do the Simplest Thing That Could Possibly Work, You Aren't Gonna Need It, and Once and Only Once (these are explained in Part VI).

Flexibility is the goal. Simplicity is the means to that end. Simple designs are easier to understand and to explain. Simple code is easier to test, maintain, and change.

XP spends comparatively little time creating designs before writing code, preferring to let the design emerge as the system grows. This is very different from most other development processes. Traditional development says *"Change is difficult, so plan for every contingency before you start."* XP says *"Change is inevitable, so plan to adapt."* By working in very small, very simple steps, continually checking to see if you're on the right track, you can identify mistakes and adapt to change very quickly.

This focus on simplicity warns against adding features that *might* be used in the future. Every unrequested feature has a cost, taking time and resources from the customer's current needs. It's a gamble that the customer will ask for a feature exactly as you imagine it now. She may never request it at all! Without the customer's input, how do you know if the code is doing anything useful? At best, you can ignore it. More often, it's just clutter—assumptions and dead code—to be worked around.

Unnecessary features complicate the system. The desire to add them comes from the fear that future changes will be difficult and expensive. While flexibility is a virtue in programming, XP achieves that flexibility through simplicity. It prefers to produce maintainable code by testing it continually, cleaning it regularly, and always seeking the simplest solution. At every stage, ask yourself "Can I simplify this code while still passing all of the tests?" You're on the right track when you can add a feature while removing more code than you write.

Adding unrequested features undermines the customer's authority. It's her job to schedule the features with the highest payoff from the business perspective. Trust her to do that.

Predicting the future is difficult. Let it come to you instead. Design only what you need when you know you need it. Rarely can anyone anticipate a future feature sufficiently to design and implement it correctly. You will know enough to create a new feature when the customer can describe it. Worry only about today's work.

A simple design supports:

- *Collective code ownership*, because of its simplicity—a complex system encourages specialization. (See "Developer Practice 3: Adopt Collective Code Ownership.")
- *Refactoring*, because smaller changes are easier to see and to implement. (See "Coding Practice 2: Refactor Mercilessly.")
- *Testing*, because simpler code is easier to test. (See "Developer Practice 1: Adopt Test-Driven Development.")

A simple design requires:

- *Good communication between developers and the customer*, to identify the necessary features.
- *Confidence*, for the whole team to believe that you can adapt to change.
- *The rare ability to recognize simplicity*, or at least the willingness to keep trying.

Coding Practice 2: Refactor Mercilessly

Goal: to find the code's optimal design.

Refactoring is a fancy word for improving the design of existing code without changing its behavior. Think of the mathematical idea of factoring—taking a large, complex expression apart and putting its pieces back together more simply. Refactoring similarly improves existing code to make it simpler, more concise, or more flexible.

Refactor your code regularly. After making a test pass, refactor the new code. After finishing a task, take a few moments to do a little house cleaning. Eliminate repetition. Break long methods and functions into smaller ones. Clarify variable and method names. Make the most of the opportunity to simplify the code and its design. Leave the code easier to understand and easier to modify.

Discovering a potential refactoring requires human judgment. Applying that refactoring is a mechanical process. Many good IDEs (see Part VIII) support several popular refactorings. You must identify a refactoring and its target, but the editor will perform the necessary work to make or to reverse the change. Investing in and learning such a tool can pay off dramatically. Learning a few refactoring patterns will pay off even more.

XP's approach of letting design emerge as the project grows could produce unruly, brittle code if left unchecked. Regular refactoring prunes away these snarls and snags, gradually finding the optimal design. With experience, you'll notice such *"code smells"* as hardcoded constants, repetition, and unclear variable and method names. After you complete a task and verify that it works, clean up a couple of the design issues you noticed.

Refactoring should simplify the overall design. Refactoring should change only the structure of code, leaving its external behavior untouched. Ideally, a test that passes before a refactoring will also pass after that refactoring *without modification*. By relying on tests, you can simplify your code while retaining its necessary behavior.

Every refactoring has a goal. Many are small and incremental, building on each other. Some add complexity to enable new features or further refactorings. Breaking one long method into smaller methods can reveal further simplifications and unifications.

It's common to delete code while refactoring, as you discover that multiple tasks have similar implementations. By refactoring after each task, you keep the amount of duplication low. A little regular cleaning can prevent a Herculean effort. Suppose your project is to write a simulation game. You might notice that the code that processes money in a candy machine is similar to the code that processes money in a pinball machine. A good refactoring will put the similar code in just one place, leaving specific details with each machine. If a soda machine is added later, it can probably use the same code.

Refactoring regularly requires discipline. Resist the temptation to put off until tomorrow the improvements you can see today. Even writing them down for later can lessen their importance. The better factored the code, the faster you can work. Don't spend all of your time looking for the best possible design, though. Make it work, make it simpler, and move on. Balance refactoring with adding features for the customer.

The dedication required to refactor *mercilessly* can achieve remarkable results in small steps. However, you may occasionally see the opportunity to simplify the architecture dramatically with an afternoon of dedicated refactoring. In this case, add a task or ask the customer for permission. Be prepared to demonstrate real business value; dramatically simplifying the architecture all at once should be rare.

Coding is like cooking. If you let pots and pans pile up, you'll eventually run out of clean dishes and counter space. By washing as you go, you'll always be ready to cook at a moment's notice. (It seems that many projects would rather build a new house when the sink gets full than fill the dishwasher.) Wading through messy and fragile code is disheartening. Working with clean and simple code is a joy.

Merciless refactoring supports:

- *Simple design*, by improving it regularly. (See "Coding Practice 1: Code and Design Simply.")
- *Disciplined coding*, because a clean house is easier to keep clean.

Merciless refactoring requires:

- *Discipline*, to find and to perform potential refactorings whenever possible.

- *Comprehensive tests*, to prove that the *behavior* of the code remains the same across refactorings. (See "Developer Practice 1: Adopt Test-Driven Development.")

- *Collective code ownership*, to enable you to refactor any part of the system that needs it. (See "Developer Practice 3: Adopt Collective Code Ownership.")

- *Coding standards*, to govern the types of changes that the team expects. (See "Coding Practice 3: Develop Coding Standards.")

Coding Practice 3: Develop Coding Standards

Goal: to communicate ideas clearly through code.

Develop coding standards to help developers communicate through their code. Code is the primary form of communication within the project. Feature requests and charts will come and go, but the project lives or dies with the software. As long as someone maintains it, it lives.

Coding standards are conventions. They're almost conversational techniques. They describe your best practices. Like a real conversation, they come from the input of everyone involved. They also evolve with the project—the standards at the middle of a project may have diverged from the standards at the beginning. Evaluate them by how well they communicate the intent of the code. Allow them to change—as your project progresses, you may invent new style ideas that provide greater clarity.

The best coding standards are guidelines, not commandments. They represent your project's shared values, both symbolically and in reality. When necessary, they can be suspended. Reasonable and thoughtful developers know when rules can be broken.

Coding standards save time. When confronted with code in an unfamiliar style, re-indenting is the natural response, followed by revising it with your preferred idioms. A team-wide coding standard will avoid this busywork—you'll adjust to the team style, concentrating on the ideas behind the code instead of the symbols that represent them. Ideally, any coder should be able to modify existing code in the same way as would its original author. Working together is easier when everyone agrees on brace placement and follows good naming guidelines. Refactoring is easier to see and to automate for code of a single style.

Many languages have existing style guides. Start there, and then adapt them to your current project.* Agree on the simple issues first, such as brace placement and tab stops, and stick with it, lest these holy wars consume too much time. Naming standards and API conventions are more important because they're harder to quantify and benefit from more direction. Agreeing on a naming standard can prevent the same method from being written multiple times. Above all, let the entire team reach a compromise.

A good source code control system can run scripts against the code when it's checked in. This allows automatic checking of simple coding rules. Some projects also add standards compliance checks to their test suite.

Coding standards should be short and memorable. Give advice, and then explain the underlying reason for the decision. Allow the standards to educate new developers about your team values, not just on the type of code to write. A well-written example is far more effective than a list of rules, and these standards will flow naturally as people work with the code.

* Resist the temptation to apply your standards to other languages or other groups. Their conversations will be different.

Coding standards support:

- *Refactoring*, because it is easier to see and to automate potential refactorings when all of the code has a similar style. (See "Coding Practice 2: Refactor Mercilessly.")

- *Pair programming*, because developers can focus on the intent of the code rather than style issues. (See "Developer Practice 2: Practice Pair Programming.")

- *Collective code ownership*, because the code has the fingerprints of the team rather than individual developers. (See "Developer Practice 3: Adopt Collective Code Ownership.")

Coding standards require:

- *Developer teamwork*, to set aside habits and preferences in favor of clear communication.

- *Occasional review*, to ensure that the existing standards communicate the shared values and intent of the code sufficiently.

- *Pair programming*, to help ensure that all new code adheres to the standards. (See "Developer Practice 2: Practice Pair Programming.")

Coding Practice 4: Develop a Common Vocabulary

Goal: to communicate ideas about code clearly.

Develop a common vocabulary to describe your project as it evolves. This vocabulary will likely come from a metaphor with well-understood relationships. It may be silly, such as describing a message delivery system as a doughnut factory, with dough hoppers to produce the raw text, a deep fryer to encode files, a sprinkle machine to add headers, and a conveyor belt to send messages. It may be more serious, like a letter put in an envelope, addressed, and dropped into a mailbox. It's often helpful to stretch reality to find the right imagery; metaphors too close to the problem offer little insight.

Your vocabulary should describe each major component in the project. Keep it expressive and approachable because you'll share it with the customer. A good vocabulary should evoke word pictures. An excellent vocabulary can speak to people who've never read a UML diagram (e.g., the customer).

Regularly review your vocabulary to ensure it represents the project accurately. As the project matures, it will take on new characteristics. Your understanding of the architecture will change. You'll discover ambiguities and limitations as you talk to the customer and your managers. Change your metaphor as necessary. Simplify. Clarify.

A good vocabulary clarifies and explains. It is fertile with possibilities for new descriptions. It's easy to add new elements to describe new components, and it's obvious how the new pieces fit into the existing system. It has room to grow.

Like good writing, your vocabulary should be as small as possible while still covering the subject. A memorable metaphor beats a meticulous map. Be concise. Describe just the features of the system that actually exist. Add a stamp to the letter metaphor only when you need it to describe a new feature.

A shared vocabulary supports:

- *Collective code ownership*, because all developers have a picture of the entire system in their heads. (See "Developer Practice 3: Adopt Collective Code Ownership.")
- *Constant customer communication*, because it allows technical and business users to communicate with a common language. (See "Business Practice 1: Add a Customer to the Team.")
- *A simple design*, because a complex design is harder to describe. (See "Coding Practice 1: Code and Design Simply.")

A shared vocabulary requires:

- *Simple design*, to be described simply. (See "Coding Practice 1: Code and Design Simply.")

Developer Practices

On all but the smallest projects, developers must work together. The more smoothly you can do this, the greater your chance of success. Everyone contributes to the project, so XP devotes several practices to improving teamwork. These practices reinforce good programming habits by guiding less experienced developers and keeping everyone on track.

Developer Practice 1: Adopt Test-Driven Development

Goal: to prove that the code works as it should.

Adopt test-driven development. Write a test that fails. Write code to pass the test. Check that the test passes. Refactor the code. Automate your tests. Keep them passing. Use failing tests to prompt you to write code. This cycle produces a natural rhythm of rapid feedback.

Traditional testing is difficult, especially when you're testing your own code. There is tremendous pressure for success. Writing a test that fails can be disheartening. It's easy to rush through tests after you're "done," expecting that everything works correctly. Test-driven development is different. Tests are supposed to fail; there's no code yet to make them pass! Writing the code to pass the test will give you a nice sense of accomplishment.

A feature is finished when all of its tests pass. Untested features do not exist. "Known issues" reduce that sense of immediacy, making debugging more difficult. Therefore, test failures should reflect only the last few minutes of changes to the system. Expected failures open the door for developers and customers to adopt the idea that unexpected behaviors and half-finished features are acceptable. A building with just one broken window will soon have many broken windows.[*]

---

[*] See Bill Venners' interview with Andy Hunt and Dave Thomas at *http://www.artima.com/intv/fixit2.html*.

Run your tests at every opportunity. The immediate feed-back from running the tests gives a nice boost of confidence. Everything's okay. Run your tests before and after every change. The less time between introducing a defect and noticing it, the less time and effort you'll spend debugging. Finding a bug in the last change is pretty easy. Finding a bug in the last five lines of code is even easier. Use a good test framework (see Part VIII); amazing amounts of software development resources have solved the most common problems, making testing so easy that it's as natural as compiling.

Automate your tests. Use a good test framework. The less time and work it takes to run the tests and interpret the results, the quicker the test-driven cycle. You should be able to receive accurate feedback about the state of the entire project at any point. Human testers may forget a test occa-sionally or misinterpret a result, but an automated test suite will not. Computers rarely take shortcuts or slack off as lunchtime nears.

Tests must pass or fail unambiguously. Good tests explore one thing at a time. They are easy to run, run as fast as possi-ble, and stay out of the way when they pass. When tests fail, they should fail dramatically and noisily, giving sufficient information to track down the failure. Occasional, mysteri-ous failures will sap your confidence. Simple tests are much easier to debug than complex tests.

Tests fall into two categories. *Unit tests* (or *developer tests*) explore the behavior of individual pieces of code and check implementations. *Acceptance tests* (or *customer tests*) verify that the requested features match the business requirements and expectations of the customer.

Write a unit test before writing the code to be tested. If you're fixing a bug, write a test that exposes the bug before you fix it. Exercise the proper behavior of the feature. The test must fail to validate that the test *can* fail. Next, write the simplest code that could possibly pass the test. Run the test again. It will pass unless the code or the test has a bug. When the test passes, refactor.

For example, suppose your task is to make the simulation's candy machine give the correct change. First, choose a good method name, such as give_change. The most obvious test is to see if this function exists.* Write and run the test. It should fail. Add the method with an empty body. The test should now pass.

Next, check that the method returns nothing if no change is due. Test the method's return value. Depending on your language, it may pass or fail. If it fails, return zero explicitly. The test should now pass.

Next, test that the method returns the appropriate amount of change when it's due. Feed the machine 60 cents and purchase a 50-cent item. give_change should return 10 cents. The test will fail because the method returns nothing. Add code to subtract the amount due from the amount paid. The test should now pass.

There's one obvious test left: the case where the machine has not yet received enough money. Feed the machine 25 cents and select a 40-cent item. Test that asking for change returns nothing, not –15 cents. The test should fail because there is no code yet to handle this case. (If the test passes, you've been working ahead.) Add code to return nothing if the amount paid is less than the amount due. All tests should pass now.

This process can seem counterintuitive, but it works well for growing systems. The tight test-driven cycle creates a natural rhythm of feedback loops, producing a comprehensive test suite that explores the essential behavior of the code. You may discover that you can work in larger steps, but don't work ahead of your tests. Stay within the cycle. If you're not

---

* In dynamic languages such as Perl, Python, or Ruby, the code can compile even if the function is defined later. In a static language, the test probably won't compile unless the method is defined.

catching enough bugs, test more. If you're spending too much time testing, test a little less. You'll find the right amount and level of testing with experience.

Every unique and identifiable piece of the system deserves its own test case. These tests show that the code works as you expect. They probe the limits of expected and unexpected uses and serve as a guide for future changes. Well-written unit tests can also serve as examples of how to use the code. Adopting the fail-code-pass cycle tends to produce systems that are simpler (simpler code is easier to test), better designed (writing tests first requires that you consider good interfaces), and more robust. As defects are introduced, they can be detected and corrected quickly.

Test-driven development forces you to work in small steps. A failing test provides the impetus to add (or sometimes remove) code. This is most obvious with APIs. To test an interface properly, you must consider how it should work before you write it. Instead of letting the implementation determine the interface, the external interface, driven by the tests, suggests the internal implementation. Your test is the interface's first user. By testing it before writing it, you'll generally make it simpler and easier to use.

Isolated testing has a drawback, however. While individual units may pass all of their tests, the complete system may fail when run as a whole. *Integration tests* can fill in the gap by checking to see that all of the pieces fit together well. Run the integration tests before and after committing a new feature to verify that any changes continue to work with the rest of the system.

Acceptance tests come directly from the customer's requirements. For every request, work with the customer to write automated acceptance tests to prove that the request has been implemented successfully. When all of the acceptance tests pass, the work is complete. Before the customer accepts a release, she should run the full acceptance test suite to verify that everything works as she expects. To measure your progress, graph the number of passing acceptance tests over time.

Tests are a safety net. They provide you immediate feedback about the project. They assure you that the current code is sufficient to implement the required features. They allow refactoring and change without fear.

Test-driven development supports:

- *Refactoring*, as developers catch unintended behavioral changes. (See "Coding Practice 2: Refactor Mercilessly.")
- *Frequent releases*, as developers ensure that the system is kept in prime working condition. (See "Business Practice 3: Release Regularly.")
- *Collective code ownership*, as tests serve as both documentation and a safety net for future development. (See "Developer Practice 3: Adopt Collective Code Ownership.")

Test-driven development requires:

- *Positive peer pressure*, for developers to overcome the initial shock of test-driven development and to continue testing even when it seems difficult.
- *Clear customer communication*, to identify what the acceptance tests should cover. (See "Business Practice 1: Add a Customer to the Team.")

Developer Practice 2: Practice Pair Programming

Goal: to spread knowledge, experience, and ideas.

Program in pairs. When you start a task, ask another developer to work with you. Pairs generally work together for just one task, perhaps an entire afternoon, and then form other pairs with new partners. This spreads the knowledge of the system throughout the whole team.

In pair programming, two developers work together to accomplish a single task. The person with the keyboard—the *driver*—focuses on the details of the task. He thinks tactically. The other person—the *navigator*—keeps the entire project in mind, ensuring that the task fits into the project as a whole and keeping track of the team guidelines. She thinks strategically. Both roles are important, and both roles are fluid. When inspiration strikes you, drive. Your partner will navigate. Change roles as necessary.

Pair programming produces code through conversation. Ask each other "What is the next step we must accomplish?", "How can we test it?", "What is the simplest code we could possibly write to pass the test?", and "How can we refactor the new code?" At each step of the test-code-refactor cycle, collaborate to find the best solution.

Pairs reinforce good programming habits, with each partner exerting positive peer pressure on the other. Having a partner present reduces the temptation to skip testing, refactoring, or simplifying. Two brains on a task and two sets of eyes on the code produce fewer bugs, leading to cleaner code that fits the team coding standards. Spend a little more time on communication while you code. It will produce higher quality code that needs much less debugging.

Working in pairs and keeping the coding standards in mind also lessens the temptation to rewrite code for its own sake. During each task, the navigator always keeps the big picture in mind, continually asking whether larger changes are necessary. The tests serve both as documentation and as a guide to keep the system working to its full potential.

Pairing is highly informal. Pairings happen naturally, exploring the entire possible combination of developers. XP calls this *promiscuous pairing*. Rather than working in assigned pairs, spread your knowledge around the team, learning from and teaching everyone else. In some situations, however, it's necessary to pair more aggressively, if cliques are forming or if pairs are becoming stale. Creating unlikely pairs can be very revealing.

Pairing can be uncomfortable at first, but it supports most of the other practices. For example, it decreases feelings of individual code ownership—code is shared from the start. Though a highly disciplined developer may practice the test-code-refactor cycle on his own, most developers need the external motivation that pairing provides. Many developers grow to enjoy pairing so much they cannot imagine developing without it.

Pair programming is an investment in continual training. This applies to people new to the project as well as developers with less programming experience. A junior developer can learn from a senior developer and vice versa. Also, if you're familiar with a technique or technology, you can demonstrate it to your partner. You have the opportunity to explain your assumptions, goals, and history, while your partner has the opportunity to ask questions that may shed new light on the project. As a rule, peers tend to mentor each other.

Pair programming supports:

- *Collective code ownership*, as two people create each line of code. (See "Developer Practice 3: Adopt Collective Code Ownership.")

- *Comprehensive testing*, providing positive peer pressure to follow your team guidelines. (See "Developer Practice 1: Adopt Test-Driven Development.")

- *Simple design and refactoring*, because two people are likely to come up with better ideas than one person alone. (See "Coding Practice 1: Code and Design Simply" and "Coding Practice 2: Refactor Mercilessly.")

- *Good development practices*, keeping developers focused on productive behaviors.

- *A greater sense of teamwork and high morale*, as you learn to enjoy and to respect working together.

Pair programming requires:

- *Facilities designed for pairing,* to allow two programmers to sit and work together at one workstation. (See "The Bullpen" in Part IV.)
- *Developers willing to try pair programming.*
- *Managers willing to try pair programming,* to produce better code with less overall effort.
- *Coding standards,* to allow developers to code with the same voice. (See "Coding Practice 3: Develop Coding Standards.")

Developer Practice 3: Adopt Collective Code Ownership

Goal: to spread the responsibility for the code to the whole team.

Adopt collective code ownership, where the entire codebase belongs to the whole team. Any developer is free to change any piece of the code as needed to complete a task. This allows you to move at your natural pace. Write the appropriate tests, write the necessary code, and run the full test suite to verify that your changes make sense.

The alternative to collective code ownership is individual code ownership, where individual developers have complete responsibility for certain subsystems. To make a change in one piece, you must ask permission of its owner. She may be the only person who understands that code. She may be on vacation, get hit by a bus, or be so swamped with other work that she has no time to make your changes. Collective code ownership gives you the power to make necessary changes yourself, wherever they are needed.

Collective code ownership reinforces the code review goals of the other practices. Because any other pair may (and will) someday work on your current code, adhere to coding standards. Keep it clean. Ideally, you should be able to read any section of code just as you would have written it. If you notice any code that can be improved, refactor it.

Collective code ownership requires teamwork. Pair programming makes two people responsible for each line of code in the system, increasing the sense of team ownership. Coding standards provide a vocabulary of coding idioms. The customer's feature requests guide what to write.

Effective collective code ownership requires frequent, small integrations. The smaller the changes and the more often the updates, the closer each pair will be to the current state of the code. Put another way, a pair helps a new feature to be born and then immediately releases it to the care of the entire team. Features are maintained, not owned.

Collective code ownership enables larger refactorings. As the system develops, greater simplifications, clarifications, and reuses become clear. When you see the opportunity to refactor, take it, even if it means changing code beyond the current task. Your design will evolve, one step at a time.

Collective code ownership supports:

- *Refactoring*, allowing any pair to make any changes to any part of the system. (See "Coding Practice 2: Refactor Mercilessly.")
- *Pair programming*, to help partners switch easily. (See "Developer Practice 2: Practice Pair Programming.")

Collective code ownership requires:

- *Coding standards*, so that the style of the code is consistent across developers. (See "Coding Practice 3: Develop Coding Standards.")
- *Comprehensive testing*, to ensure that risky changes can be detected and fixed rapidly. (See "Developer Practice 1: Adopt Test-Driven Development.")

- *Frequent integration*, so that all pairs have access to the freshest code. (See "Developer Practice 4: Integrate Continually.")
- *A shared vocabulary*, to explain the place of each piece of the code within the whole system. (See "Coding Practice 4: Develop a Common Vocabulary.")

Developer Practice 4: Integrate Continually

Goal: to reduce the impact of adding new features.

Integrate continually, merging new tasks and tests into the main source code repository as soon as they're completed. Run the tests to verify that the new code fits well into the system. Fix any errors—check code into the repository only when the test suite passes fully. Check out the latest code frequently.

Continual integration keeps everyone on the same page. By keeping tasks small, pairs can integrate their work after a few minutes or a few hours—everyone can work on the freshest possible working code. Staying close to the main source tree avoids the pain of playing catch-up after weeks or months away. Code cleanups and other enhancements made by one pair are only an integration away for everyone else.

Integration must be simple. Just run the test suites, merge, and commit the code. It must be quick and painless. Automate as much as you can. You'll be integrating often. The rest of the team should not have to wait for you to finish. Having short tasks helps by producing fewer changes to merge.

Developer machines should also be stateless. Any code or artifact necessary for integrating or building should be in source control. You should be able to switch to a different computer, check out the latest code, and start a new task. Some teams pass a token to mark integration rights. This helps to prevent collisions—if you have the stuffed animal, you can integrate. Other teams use a dedicated machine. If you're sitting there, you can integrate.

Continual integration avoids the temptation to let tasks slide between days. At the end of a day, either integrate your current work or discard it. Tasks that run longer than their estimates often indicate unanticipated difficulties. Perhaps it required more work than you expected or things just don't make sense right now. Rather than working late, building up frustration, and being tempted to cut corners, go home. The task will be there in the morning. Delete the code, but keep what you've learned while writing it. Get a good night's sleep and start over in the morning. Throwing out work can seem scary, but keeping tasks small and manageable (see "Business Practice 2: Play the Planning Game") reduces the risks of starting over too often.

Continual integration tightens the feedback loops within the whole system. Small, frequent adjustments will have fewer collisions than large, dramatic changes—and are easier to correct if collisions occur. By integrating only simple, well-tested code that adds one feature at a time, you can keep the project in a releasable state. After any integration, the customer can run the acceptance tests for the completed features. If they pass, she can accept delivery.

Integrating continually supports:

- *Refactoring*, by making the latest code from other developers always available. (See "Coding Practice 2: Refactor Mercilessly.")
- *Releasing regularly*, because the system is always well-tested and ready to be accepted by the customer. (See "Business Practice 3: Release Regularly.")

Integrating continually requires:

- *A collective source code repository*, to hold the master source.
- *Comprehensive testing*, to judge the health of the system. (See "Developer Practice 1: Adopt Test-Driven Development.")
- *A quick test suite*, to speed up integrations.

- *The planning game*, to divide the work into small pieces. (See "Business Practice 2: Play the Planning Game.")
- *Working at a sustainable pace*, to know how much time to invest in a task in a day. (See "Business Practice 4: Work at a Sustainable Pace.")

Business Practices

Building a successful software project requires far more than just coding. A beautiful, elegant, and comprehensively tested project is useless unless it meets the customer's actual needs. Furthermore, the customer has finite time limits. You have finite resources. Exceeding either or both increases the chance of failure. Quality is also up to the customer, but developers should make the technical risks of reducing quality clear. The customer must decide if having a good-enough feature by a certain date is more important than having perfect software later.

XP is designed to minimize risk. Including the customer in the team improves communication between customers and developers. It's easier to ask the customer what she wants directly instead of making guesses. Observing the project regularly allows the customer to guide the project based on immediate feedback. Dividing the project's responsibilities along business and technical lines allows customers and developers to make the decisions they're best qualified to make.

Business Practice 1: Add a Customer to the Team

Goal: to address business concerns accurately and directly.

Add a customer to the team. XP calls this the *Whole Team*. The customer provides a business perspective as an actual user of the software. Regular, reliable, and rapid communication between technical and business people improves confidence, reduces guesswork and misunderstandings, and produces the desired results more quickly.

The customer should work closely with you. Ideally, she will work alongside the developers. She writes story cards and is always available to answer questions. The closer the customer is to the rest of the team, the better. Make it as easy as possible to go directly to the source of business knowledge— if possible, make it easier to turn around to ask the customer a question than to assume the answer.

While the customer has many XP duties, they will consume only part of her normal work week. For the first release or two, she may find herself writing and rewriting feature requests and explaining business concepts to the developers. As the project continues, she will have more time to devote to her regular duties. Including the customer in the project from the start, to set goals and give feedback, will pay off by preventing bugs and large-scale rework.

Besides setting development goals and serving as a resource for business questions, the customer writes and runs acceptance tests based on her story cards. These may initially be very simple, manual tests, run while flipping through the stack of completed cards. Like programmer tests, customer tests should be automated as soon as possible. Work with the customer to produce these tests from her feature requests. When you've finished a feature, she must verify that its tests all pass. She may run these tests at any point to receive immediate feedback about the team's current progress.

The customer provides a business perspective to evaluate the project. She has the responsibility for adjusting the project's scope. When you discover that you've committed to too few or too many stories for the current schedule, ask the customer to add or to remove work based on its business value.

This flexibility helps you to stick to a regular schedule, keeping the software in working order. It's better to deliver software that fills the customer's most important needs on time than to delay the software to add less important features. Allow the customer to decide what is most valuable.

Many projects will need to modify these rules slightly, if having an onsite customer is impossible. The whole team can regularly ask, "How can we change our habits to be even more effective?" Some teams elect a customer proxy to act as an authoritative, single point of contact for business goals and knowledge. However you find a customer, she must speak with one voice. Someone must take final responsibility for making business decisions. The customer must set the project's goals and schedule. Close communication with your customer is essential to your success.

A customer in the team supports:

- *The planning game*, by writing story cards and scheduling the iteration's features. (See "Business Practice 2: Play the Planning Game.")
- *Acceptance testing*, by writing and running the tests. (See "Developer Practice 1: Adopt Test-Driven Development.")
- *Regular releases*, by adjusting the iteration schedule as necessary.

A customer in the team requires:

- *An initial investment in the project*, to convince the customer to join the team.
- *A common vocabulary*, to improve communication between the customer and the developers. (See "Coding Practice 4: Develop a Common Vocabulary.")

Business Practice 2: Play the Planning Game

Goal: to schedule the most important work.

Play the planning game to produce and to refine your schedule. XP uses the phrase *Planning Game* to describe the give and take process of deciding which features to implement in what order. The goal of the planning game is to maximize the value of features produced.

XP schedules are based around the *iteration*. An iteration is a snapshot of the entire development cycle. The customer requests features. The team plans them. They're implemented, tested, and delivered. The whole process takes one to four weeks before it starts again.

XP divides planning responsibilities along two lines. Business people make business decisions, deciding how to allocate resources and set the priority of the features. What should be done? What is the value and risk of each feature? Which features are more important than others? Technical people make technical decisions, choosing technologies and implementation details. How should a feature be implemented? What kind of technical risk does each feature have? How long will it take to implement the feature?

The planning game takes place at the start of each release. The customer requests features by writing story cards. A *story card* is an index card that contains a short feature request. Stories describe the the use and behavior of the feature rather than its implementation. An example story card might read, "Players should be able to ride a roller coaster."

From these story cards, the developers produce estimates, based on an imaginary unit of time called an *ideal hour*. An ideal hour represents the amount of work you could accomplish if you were completely productive, completely focused, and completely undisturbed. These estimates correspond to the number of ideal hours in an iteration.

Armed with story cards and their estimates, the customer chooses stories to fill the next iteration. She can add stories until their estimates meet or exceed the amount of time in the iteration. The remaining stories go in a pile marked "future." Consequently, stories should be much smaller than one iteration. Ask the customer to split stories as necessary.

Developers next produce task cards from the story cards. Each *task card* represents a development task necessary to implement the story. Every story will have at least one task card. Tasks should be sufficiently detailed that you can start the test-code-refactor cycle to gauge when the task is finished. An example task for the simulation might be "Create a HamburgerStand class that can sell food." Each task card also includes an estimate of the amount of time needed to complete the task. Tasks generally represent a few hours of work, rarely exceeding an afternoon or a full day.

Story cards must demonstrate a recognizable business value. This can be a feature immediately visible to end users, such as adding a hamburger stand to the simulation. It can also be an infrastructure task that the developers have convinced the customer to schedule, such as migrating to a new version of the database. Stories must also be testable. The acceptance tests explore the behavior the story describes.

Story and task cards serve as signposts to measure progress within an iteration. The acceptance tests reveal which stories are complete. Comparing the time remaining in an iteration to the estimates of outstanding tasks approximates the amount of work that can be finished by the end of the iteration. If you outperform your estimates, the customer can add extra tasks. If you underperform, the customer can defer stories until later iterations. In practice, your estimates will rapidly improve to a state of sufficient accuracy.

Occasionally, you may ask the customer to add story cards. This usually marks the need for a critical piece of infrastructure, or plans for an extra amount of refactoring. Developers assess the value of the story and its technical risk. The customer evaluates and schedules these cards as usual. Adding cards should be rare. If the customer's story cards leave gaps, work with her to clarify them. Any story cards you suggest *must* have an obvious benefit to the customer.

The planning game supports:

- *A simple design*, because only the features the customer has scheduled will be implemented. (See "Coding Practice 1: Code and Design Simply.")

- *Acceptance testing*, because the story cards identify what the customer wants to see. (See "Developer Practice 1: Adopt Test-Driven Development.")

- *Regular releases*, because iteration planning allows short, predictable iterations. (See "Business Practice 3: Release Regularly.")

The planning game requires:

- *An active customer*, to write story cards and to set priorities. (See "Business Practice 1: Add a Customer to the Team.")

- *Mutual respect*, for customers to believe developer estimates and for developers to believe customer stories and priorities.

Business Practice 3: Release Regularly

Goal: to return the customer's investment often.

Release regularly. At the end of each iteration, after the software passes all acceptance tests, release the software to the customer. Keep iterations short—from one to four weeks long. Keep your feedback loops short. Allow regular, small adjustments.

A short release cycle quickly starts to return on the customer's investment. With every release, the customer receives her most valuable features. You can respond to her feedback rapidly—scheduling and implementing her changes in the next iteration. She'll receive a steady flow of features, adapted to her actual current needs.

Regular releases deliver bug fixes well. While critical bug fixes can be delivered immediately, less severe bugs can be scheduled as normal stories and included in the next appropriate iteration. The customer can decide to work around a bug for a few days if she knows that it will be fixed within the next iteration.

Regular, small releases are less painful. You will receive more and better feedback by working in a scale of days, not years. The customer will need to adapt to fewer big changes by receiving smaller, more frequent changes. Though releases can be painful in traditional software projects, XP provides strong pressure to optimize and to automate releases by releasing often. Make the process as easy as possible.

Regular releases provide frequent opportunities for evaluation. The customer has concrete, working code as a progress report. Business users know that their priorities dictate the feature set. They can frequently adjust the schedule to changing business conditions. You will see what succeeds and fails immediately, and can adjust your estimates and practices accordingly.

Regular releases also allow the customer a final option. She can end the project at any time she feels she has recouped her investment. If the software is kept in a releasable state and stories have been prioritized properly, the software always represents the best possible value for her investment.

Regular releases support:

- *The planning game*, by allowing the customer to change the schedule regularly. (See "Business Practice 2: Play the Planning Game.")

Regular releases require:

- *Simple design*, to keep iterations short and manageable. (See "Coding Practice 1: Code and Design Simply.")
- *Comprehensive testing*, to ensure that all of the code works. (See "Developer Practice 1: Adopt Test-Driven Development.")
- *Continual integration*, to keep the code in a releasable state. (See "Developer Practice 4: Integrate Continually.")
- *The planning game*, to set priorities for the current iteration. (See "Business Practice 2: Play the Planning Game.")

Business Practice 4: Work at a Sustainable Pace

Goal: to go home tired, but not exhausted.

Work at a sustainable pace. Everyone has a natural level of productivity. It will vary from person to person, but everyone has a limited amount of physical, mental, and creative energy. Every hour of work costs energy. Sleep, family activities, and recreation replenish your reserves. Pushing your limits is counterproductive.

Your team's choices tend to become habits—especially the hours you work. Working overtime to complete an iteration instead of reducing its scope can artificially inflate your velocity, unless you factor overtime into the number of real hours you work. Your velocity must be accurate to schedule the next iteration. Overcommitting due to overtime exacerbates the problem—you're promising more than you could actually deliver in the previous iteration.

As soon as you discover that you have more tasks than fit in the time remaining, adjust your scope. First, shuffle tasks between developers. Perhaps someone has more available time. If that doesn't solve the problem, the customer must choose stories to delay. Address schedule changes by reducing scope. Keep the number of working hours and the iteration length constant. With regular releases and the customer adjusting the schedule, the software will still provide the best possible value at any point in time. There's always a next iteration.

Occasionally, scope change may not address the issue—for example, when fixing a critical bug. If you must work overtime today, you cannot work overtime next week. If you find yourself constantly needing to work late, evaluate the actions that led to this point and fix the situation by changing your development practices.

Working at a sustainable pace will keep your productivity high. A tired programmer is tempted to take shortcuts and is susceptible to lapses in judgment and simple errors of fatigue. By taking regular breaks throughout the day, stopping at the end of a normal workday, and resting on weekends, you'll be more productive over the long term than if you stayed late and worked weekends. Also, developers who know that their project can wait overnight or over the weekend will have higher morale than developers who perceive they need to work longer and longer hours just to catch up.

Working at a sustainable pace means more than avoiding overtime; it means taking on only as many projects as you can handle. By removing the obstacles to productivity (long meetings, excessive documentation, communication overhead), you can concentrate on what is important and avoid unnecessary tasks.

Vacation and play are important. Demonstrate their importance by having a party on the afternoon when an iteration ends. Allow time for vacations and personal days when planning an iteration. Adjust the number of available work units accordingly. Pair programming, collective code ownership, and test-driven development build up a technical credit that allows the team to work effectively even if multiple developers are out of the office.

Working at a sustainable pace is made easier by:

- *The planning game*, to schedule features by priority. (See "Business Practice 2: Play the Planning Game.")
- *An onsite customer*, to make scope changes. (See "Business Practice 1: Add a Customer to the Team.")
- *Integrating continually*, to minimize the amount of time you spend away from the main code tree. (See "Developer Practice 4: Integrate Continually.")
- *Regular releases*, to give the customer confidence that new features will arrive at a reliable rate. (See "Business Practice 3: Release Regularly.")

PART III

XP Events

Iterations are crucial to XP. They're independent and self-contained—smaller, faster versions of the traditional software development cycle. Iterations lessen risk by taking on less work. Iterations allow rapid feedback and improved flexibility because of their shorter length. If you can work in small steps, you can refine your decisions as your ultimate goals become clearer.

Iteration Planning

A project's primary purpose will remain constant—to produce the most valuable software for the customer. The customer's values will change over time. Every iteration offers the chance to adjust the schedule to match those values. The *iteration planning meeting* brings the customer and developers together to reassess the project and to schedule the upcoming iteration. This meeting is *customer driven*. The customer sets priorities for the developers, choosing features to be implemented and delivered during the iteration.

Stories and Tasks

The customer presents his desired features as story cards (see "Story Cards" in Part IV). Story cards communicate the customer's specifications to the developers. The customer has decided what must be done. Developers then estimate how long it will take. In this sense, iteration planning is also *developer driven*. These discussions produce task cards (see "Task

Cards" in Part IV), one for each step required to implement the story.*

All stories should represent a few days worth of work at most. When first described, some stories may be too large or too difficult to estimate. Ask the customer to elaborate or to split one story into smaller stories. Over time, everyone will develop a sense for what makes a good story.

As the project progresses, business changes can affect pending stories. The customer should re-evaluate them as necessary. Tasks can also change if their stories change or if existing code can be reused for the story. Remember to re-evaluate any tasks that might have changed when planning the iteration.

For example, one story may be to add a balloon vendor to the simulation. One of its tasks might be to create a new WanderingVendor class. If a story to add a souvenir vendor had been added in the previous iteration, the balloon vendor story could probably reuse some of that work; thus, the WanderingVendor task would be moot.

Estimates and Schedules

Developers estimate how much time each story and task will take. Story estimates help the customer schedule stories for an iteration. Task estimates help developers schedule tasks within an iteration. These estimates are simply educated guesses—as honest as possible, but measured in ideal, not actual, time. This measures the actual work involved, ignoring interruptions, meetings, and the normal ebb and flow of development. These estimates include the time necessary for the test-code-refactor cycle as well as integration. An ideal hour represents at least one clock hour.

---

* XP has no separate design stage, preferring to mix design with the other practices. Writing task cards from stories requires some high-level design work. Test-driven development performs unit-level design. Refactoring is continuous design. These frequent mini design sessions add up over time.

The distinction between estimates and actual time is very important. As described in "The XP Equation" in Part I, XP prefers to adjust the schedule by adjusting the project's scope, leaving time, resources, and quality constant. To avoid confusing ideal hours with actual hours, you may prefer to measure estimates with "gummy bears" or "work units."

Story estimates help the customer set iteration priorities. The customer chooses stories by asking two questions: "What are the most valuable stories right now?" and "How much work can be accomplished in this iteration?" The customer's goal is to maximize his investment in the project.

Each story has business and technical risk,* a value, and a cost. The ideal story has a low cost and high reward. The reward may be adding an important new feature or successfully overcoming high business or technical risk. Choosing high-risk stories up front leaves easier stories for later, when there may be less time, fewer resources, or less need.

The customer selects stories to fill the number of ideal hours in the iteration. The shorter the stories, the easier they fit. Leftover stories go into a pile to be considered in the next iteration.

Every iteration has a fixed length, generally one to three actual weeks. To choose the right amount of work to schedule, the customer needs to know how much work the team can do. XP uses the principle of *Yesterday's Weather*—predicting the future by examining the recent past. Predicting that "today's weather will probably be much like yesterday's" is almost as accurate as—and much cheaper than—spending lots of money on sophisticated meteorological equipment.

A team that implemented stories estimated at 20 ideal hours in an iteration of 40 real hours will probably do the same amount of work in the next iteration. The ratio of estimated to actual work is the team's *velocity*. Because this team has a

---

* Technical risk includes implementing difficult tasks.

velocity of 0.5, the customer can select stories that add up to twenty ideal hours for the next forty-hour iteration. Individual developers have their own velocities, too.

Velocity is only a rough estimate used in planning. Instead of attempting to meet or beat a velocity of 1.0, the goal of measuring velocity is to be able to estimate accurately the amount of work you can do in an iteration. Velocity represents the relationship of estimates to actual time. It's deliberately coarsely grained; productivity flows in cycles. Stories and tasks are short enough that they can be off by an hour or two. Iterations are short enough that a task can't drag on for weeks or months. Estimates aren't so large that they're just wild guesses.

Your velocity can indicate the health of the project. Unexplained, sudden jumps may come from developers cutting corners or discovering new techniques to boost productivity. Sudden drops in velocity may indicate communication trouble, slumping morale, or unforeseen difficulties with a story.

Though some iteration planning is sequential, other parts can be done in parallel. The whole team must participate. While developers are creating task cards, the customer can be clarifying stories or writing new stories.

During an iteration, you may discover that your estimates were inaccurate. As soon as you discover that you have too much or too little work, ask the customer to adjust the iteration's scope. Keep the iteration on its schedule, but have the customer reschedule the pending stories just as he would do in the iteration planning meeting. An added story should be the next most valuable story. A delayed story should be the least valuable story in the current iteration. It can be re-evaluated for the next iteration.

A variant of the planning game removes iteration planning. The customer instead chooses specific stories he needs. The developers then add up story and task estimates to predict a delivery date. This technique can fit well with traditional development styles. It has the disadvantage of removing the feedback loop that lets the customer adjust the project's scope based on daily status reports.

The First Iteration

A project's first iteration is special; there's no code or feedback yet! XP is experiential. A new project starts small and evolves rapidly. The best thing you can do is to start learning as soon as possible.

For the first iteration only, choose several small tasks to lay a basic architecture. Plan a normal-sized iteration, but deliver as much of the end-to-end application as possible. Implement just enough functionality to kick off the next iteration. For example, the first iteration of the simulation project could have just enough code to allow the player to buy an entrance ticket, walk around the park, and buy a balloon and some cotton candy. While the finished product will do much, much more, it's okay to lay a simple foundation.

The purpose of this first iteration is to gather real data. How much work can you actually do? What is your velocity? How do the customer's needs change when he actually has working software in front of him?

Building a skeleton system allows you to explore all of the pieces that must eventually work together. You can eliminate some infrastructure risks early. For example, you may discover that your chosen database and the preferred version of your operating system don't work together. Producing a skeleton can also help you fine-tune your source control system, your build system, and your release process before any of them are too complicated to change.

Some teams choose an arbitrary velocity for the first iteration and schedule work as normal. Other teams start with a velocity of zero and continue to ask the customer for the next most important story until the end of the iteration. However you choose to start, remember to start with the most important things first.

The Iteration

The customer uses stories and iterations to make his schedule. Developers use tasks. Each developer has his own velocity, measured in the same way as the team velocity. If you implemented tasks worth 10 ideal hours in the previous iteration, you can choose tasks that add up to 10 ideal hours for this iteration. Developer velocity takes into account time spent in meetings, in planning, and in pairing with other developers.

Tackle the most important and the riskiest tasks at the start of the iteration. Invest your time and energy where it's most needed, leaving the easier tasks until the end. This will give you more time to spend implementing, integrating, and testing difficult tasks. It also tends to make the end of an iteration less stressful, in marked contrast to the crunch times that often occur in other projects.

How you choose tasks is less important than working on just one task at a time. Some teams prefer to dole out tasks during iteration planning, having each developer estimate his own tasks. Some teams estimate tasks as a team, having developers sign up for tasks at the end of the planning meeting. Still other teams have each developer choose one task at the start of an iteration. The remaining cards go on the whiteboard and developers choose from the stack as they finish.

Every developer should spend as much time pairing on one of his tasks as he spends pairing on another developer's tasks. Because tasks are short, it's easy to form and reform pairs frequently. Working in the bullpen makes it possible to switch pairs even in the middle of a task. If you get stuck in one section of the code, you can swap partners with another pair to get a fresher or more knowledgeable perspective. Keep things fluid and let teamwork happen naturally.

During the iteration, meet as a team for a brief daily *stand-up meeting* to discuss goals and progress. What did you do yesterday? What will you do today? Is anything standing in your way? To keep the meeting short, everyone stands. Some teams choose daily tasks and pairs in this meeting.

The *Tracker* (see "The Tracker" in Part V) keeps tabs on each developer's progress. This is very informal; just a couple of questions are asked every day or two: *"How many tasks have you completed?"* and *"How many ideal hours are left in your uncompleted tasks?"* Comparing the number of ideal hours to go with the number of hours left in the iteration is a good way to measure progress. If you're overwhelmed, you can give a task to another developer who is ahead of schedule. If that's not enough to get you back on schedule, ask the customer to delay a story or two.

Releasing

Releasing software is special, especially if it doesn't happen at the end of every iteration, as in the case of shrink-wrapped software development. It's a time for retrospection and celebration. Discuss the project. Throw a party, and then relax and rest up to tackle the next iteration.

The customer has several options at the end of an iteration. He can put the software into production immediately. This can be appropriate early in the project's life cycle, or with software deployed to a website or to thin clients. He can also release the software to production at specific milestones, triggered by the completion of specific features or by calendar dates. This works better in commercial software situations with quarterly or yearly releases. Short iterations help; for example, knowing that iterations always take three weeks helps to plan the delivery of major new features.

Knowing that you'll release the software soon will change how you work. To keep migrations simple, your changes must be small. On the surface, this conflicts with XP's goal of embracing change. In practice, the more frequent the releases, the smaller the migrations can be. While releasing a new version of the software every day can be distracting, an iteration period of two or three weeks strikes a good balance. The possible differences between the previous and current code are limited.

Frequent releases make it easier to learn from the current iteration and to prepare for the next iteration. What went well? What could be improved? What can you experiment with next time? Discuss this over food, as a team. If you need to change the rules, change them as a team.

Frequent releases can make meeting long-term goals difficult. In this case, the customer should keep certain milestones in mind when setting the priorities of his stories. Demo dates or media-mastering deadlines can be analyzed and scheduled just like any other business need.

Regular releases provide another feedback loop between implementing a story and delivering that feature to end users. Keep that loop as short as possible. The more often the customer can collect information on successes and frustrations, the better he can write new stories. The more often you can receive and act upon feedback from actual users, the greater the value you can demonstrate to the customer. Watching a healthy project grow and react and adjust to change is very impressive.

PART IV

Extreme Programming Artifacts

XP preaches "traveling light," preferring conversations, working code, and tests over voluminous documentation and specifications. A few physical artifacts are useful, though. In particular, the planning game (see "Business Practice 2: Play the Planning Game" in Part II) uses index cards heavily. The name gives it away; these are the game pieces by which you arrange your schedule.

Every bit of information in XP can be tracked electronically, through email, project tracking software, a spreadsheet, or a web page. In some cases, electronic tracking may be the best solution. Regular index cards work really well, though. You can write on them, stack them, tear them in pieces, and tack them to the wall. They're satisfyingly tangible, easy to carry, and require no special tools other than a pen.

Story Cards

The customer's most important tool is the story card. Story cards answer the question *what should be done?* Each card describes a desired feature of the software project in story form—a sentence or two from the customer's perspective. For example, one story may be "Avatars must be able to ride the Ferris wheel."

The customer communicates business information through story cards during the planning game. All features start as story cards. They're passed to developers, who estimate the amount of work each card represents. From the stories and estimates, the customer then schedules the stories, arranging the cards in piles to mark their status—completed, scheduled for the current iteration, or unscheduled.

The customer has complete responsibility over scheduled features—only she can create story cards. Developers may suggest stories, but the customer has final say. Along with their estimates, developers should also identify the technical risks of stories, presenting the complete technical picture to the customer. This will help her choose the correct schedule.

Every story must provide the customer with identifiable business value. This rule helps the customer to invest time and resources in the stories that matter. Any story suggested by the developers should have an obvious benefit. This will likely be technical. For example, migrating to a newer database version may make other scheduled stories easier to implement.

Each story must represent a single feature. If a story describes multiple features, ask the customer to split it. If you estimate that a story will take more than a few ideal workdays, ask the customer to split it into smaller stories. Small stories are easier to estimate and implement.

Each story should stand on its own, as far as possible. Reducing dependencies between stories is very handy. Within an iteration, you should be able to tackle scheduled stories in any order without waiting for another story to be implemented. Further, acceptance tests are more reliable progress markers; a story's tests should pass when it is finished, regardless of the status of any other story in the iteration. Stories with incomplete dependencies live in limbo. Avoid them if you can; otherwise, be aware of them.

Story cards can be imperfect. This is normal—XP makes it easy to ask for clarification. Rewrite, adjust, and split stories as necessary. Learning to communicate well takes time. After a few iterations, you'll find your rhythm.

XP expects customer needs to change with time. Start with the most important stories immediately instead of trying to identify all possible stories before planning the first iteration. Small, frequent iterations and regular releases will give you plenty of time to add new stories. Every planning game gives the opportunity to re-evaluate unscheduled stories from the future pile.

Some stories may never be implemented. Businesses change. Better ideas come along. A story may cost far more than it's worth. You may come up with better stories in the future. Writing a story card and identifying and estimating its pieces is a learning experience. Far better to invest a few minutes to realize a feature is unnecessary than to implement a feature that will never pay off.

Task Cards

Task cards are the developers' primary planning tool. They answer the question of *how should it be done?* Tasks represent the actual development steps necessary to implement a user story. Tasks for the example Ferris wheel story might include "Create a `FerrisWheel` class," "Add the Ferris wheel to the park," and "Add an `Employee` to run the Ferris wheel."

Every task card is related to a story card; all development work is prompted by customer stories. Task cards represent developer responsibilities. They're technical in nature, identifying the story's implementation details. Task cards communicate high-level design ideas between developers.

Developers write tasks during the iteration planning meeting based on the scheduled story cards. Given a story card, developers break it into tasks, sketching out its implementation details. This design is just enough to estimate the number of ideal work hours each task will cost (see "Estimates and Schedules" in Part III).

If a story is still too hard to break into tasks, or if a task is too hard to implement, experiment with a *spike solution*. In a spike solution, one or two developers write a little bit of code to explore the problem. There's no need to be formal or clean—you'll throw away the code. The purpose of this exercise is to learn just enough about the problem to be able to write task cards or to estimate the work involved.

Tasks should be small, usually just a few ideal hours. Tasks should be specific. The starting and ending points of the task should be clear. Each story needs at least one task card: writing an acceptance test for the story with the customer. The team tracker (see "The Tracker" in Part V) counts the number of completed stories and the number of pending tasks, comparing the remaining time in the iteration with the estimates of the pending tasks.

The Bullpen

Effective teamwork requires a working environment conducive to collaboration. A good team can be productive in mediocre facilities, but they'll be excellent with good facilities. This is especially true for pair programming and constant communication. Your workspace either helps or hinders cooperation.

XP recommends working in a single, wide-open room called the *bullpen* or *war room*. You need plenty of open space, tables and chairs, several whiteboards, and lots of bulletin boards, sticky notes, and index cards. Each computer must have space for two developers to sit side-by-side without bumping elbows. Small cubbies or offices are nice for personal phone calls and quiet individual work such as reading email, but the bulk of development happens in the bullpen.

Though the bullpen will buzz with activity, it should be isolated from outside noise. If possible, isolate yourselves from loud phones and heavy machinery. Pairs should be able to hear each other and other pairs. Overheard conversations often become informal brainstorming sessions, where everyone has the chance to share a bit of expertise. This may seem chaotic, but it can improve your productivity. It's easier to ask the customer a question if you can just turn around. Finding a pair programming partner takes just a few moments.

Paired developers must be able to sit next to each other, so they can switch frequently and easily between driving and navigating. It's difficult to sit together if the computer is in the corner of a cubicle. You'll switch less frequently. Both developers need to be able to work comfortably. If you need special ergonomic hardware, it's possible to use separate computers to share a desktop session, but you should still sit together.

The customer should sit with you in the bullpen. The easier it is to ask her for guidance, the more often you'll do it. Talking to her should be easier than guessing at the right answer. If developers can talk to the customer without leaving their chairs, they will.

Good lighting is important. Incandescent lights can be much gentler than harsh, fluorescent bulbs. They reduce glare and eye strain from staring at monitors for long hours. Invest in adjustable desk lamps. If necessary, turn off or disable the overhead lights.

A good bullpen needs plenty of wall space. Cover it with whiteboards—you'll use them all. Leave space for a few important charts: your team velocity and the iteration's passing acceptance tests are both handy. Some teams also post unclaimed and completed task cards on a bulletin board. This is a nice and simple way to see how things are going.

The bullpen needs powerful machines. The faster the tests run, the less painful it is to run them frequently. The faster you can integrate, the more often you will do it.

Though reworking your facilities may raise corporate eye-brows, it can dramatically help you adopt XP. It's possible to succeed even without a bullpen, though it will require more discipline. With a little creativity, you can redesign a cubicle farm into a bullpen on the cheap—just grab a screwdriver and rearrange the walls. Whether it's better to ask permission or to beg for forgiveness depends on your organization. Demonstrating XP's efficacy for a few iterations may strengthen the argument to make further changes. Successfully changing your work environment is a good predictor of future success.

PART V

Roles in Extreme Programming

Every XP project has several different roles, each with its own unique rights and responsibilities. XP attempts to improve communication between customers and developers. It accomplishes this by sharply dividing the work between the two. If you want to get any work done, you'll have to talk to each other!

XP gives developers authority to make technical decisions. This is their area of expertise. XP gives the customer authority to make business decisions. This is his area of expertise. These spheres of influence complement each other. Following these clear lines of authority will improve your chances of success.

The Customer

The customer drives the project. He defines the project and sets its goals. The more accurate his work and the more frequent his involvement, the greater the chances the project will succeed.

The customer makes business decisions. His rights and responsibilities stem from his business knowledge. He has the authority to set the project's goals and features. He must answer the questions: *"What should this feature do?"*, *"How will we know when it is done?"*, *"How much can we spend?"*, and *"When shall we start working on it?"*

The customer works closely with the developers. He writes story cards to explain and to schedule the desired features.

This answers the *what* question. He participates in the planning game to schedule stories for the next iteration. This answers the questions of *when* and *how much*. He creates and runs acceptance tests, with developer assistance, to verify that features are complete. This answers the *is it done* question.

The customer represents the end user. In a corporate, in-house project, he may be an end user. In other situations, he serves as a proxy for end users. He identifies the features users really need from their perspective. The developers will take care of the technical perspective.

The customer also represents the business interests that are paying for the project. His goal is to maximize their investment. At any point, the software should contain the most valuable features that could have been scheduled based on the available knowledge.

An XP customer relies on several pieces of information. He must understand the business problem to be solved even as it changes over time. Is a story more or less valuable now than when it was identified? Can a story be delayed, deferred, or simplified? He must be able to evaluate the project at any time. Which features are complete? How well do the completed features conform to his stories? He must understand the technical implications of a story that affect its value and its risk. Is it better to schedule a story suggested by developers before a story he wrote on his own?

XP always refers to the customer as a single person. Even if the customer is a proxy for an actual investor or far-off end users, he must speak with one voice. He holds a position of authority, with the right to say what must be done.

Customer Rights

XP recognizes several customer rights:

- *To maximize his investment*, by choosing stories to schedule in the current iteration. (See "Business Practice 2: Play the Planning Game" in Part II.)

- *To change the scope of the project to deal with schedule changes*, by selecting stories to add to or remove from an iteration if its estimates prove incorrect. (See "Business Practice 1: Add a Customer to the Team" in Part II.)

- *To determine which features to implement next*, by selecting story cards in the iteration planning meeting. (See "Business Practice 2: Play the Planning Game" in Part II.)

- *To measure the progress of the project at any time*, by running the acceptance tests. (See "Developer Practice 1: Adopt Test-Driven Development" in Part II.)

- *To stop the project at any time without losing his investment*, by keeping the software in a releasable state and continually scheduling the most worthwhile features. (See "Developer Practice 4: Integrate Continually" and "Business Practice 2: Play the Planning Game," both in Part II.)

Customer Responsibilities

XP identifies several customer responsibilities:

- *To trust the developers' technical decisions*, because they understand technology. (See "Business Practice 2: Play the Planning Game" in Part II.)

- *To analyze risk correctly*, weighing the stories against each other accurately. (See "Business Practice 2: Play the Planning Game" in Part II.)

- *To choose the stories with maximum value*, scheduling the most valuable stories that could possibly fit into the next iteration. (See "Business Practice 2: Play the Planning Game" in Part II.)

- *To provide precise stories*, enabling the developers to produce comprehensive task cards and accurate estimates. (See "Story Cards" in Part IV.)

- *To work within the team*, providing guidance and receiving feedback as quickly and accurately as possible. (See "Business Practice 1: Add a Customer to the Team" in Part II.)

The Developer

Most XP practices concern the day-to-day work of producing code. This is the job of the developer: to turn customer stories into working code.

The developer role in planning and implementing features depends on knowing and understanding technical issues. Developers create and maintain the system as it evolves. They must answer the questions: "*How will we implement it?*", "*How long will it take?*", and "*What are the risks?*"

Developers work with the customer to understand his stories. From a story, the developers decide its implementation. The developers then estimate the amount of work each story will take, based on the implementation decisions and their experience on the project so far. These estimates help the customer to schedule the most valuable work for the next iteration by answering the question of *how long*.

While creating task cards from the story cards or implementing tasks during the programming cycle, developers may identify features that depend on other features. They may also find risky features that use new technology, are poorly understood, or are otherwise complicated. Developers raise these issues with the customer, who considers them while making the schedule. In practice, these risks are rare—practicing simplicity reduces them.

Developer Rights

XP recognizes several developer rights:

- *To estimate their own work*, by giving developers authority over technical decisions. (See "Business Practice 2: Play the Planning Game" in Part II.)
- *To work a sensible and predictable schedule*, by scheduling only the amount of work that can reasonably be done. (See "Business Practice 4: Work at a Sustainable Pace" in Part II.)

- *To produce code that meets the customer's needs*, by focusing on testing, refactoring, and customer communication. (See "Developer Practice 1: Adopt Test-Driven Development" and "Coding Practice 2: Refactor Mercilessly," both in Part II.)

- *To avoid the need to make business decisions*, by allowing the customer to make them. (See "Business Practice 1: Add a Customer to the Team" in Part II.)

Developer Responsibilities

XP expects several developer responsibilities:

- *To follow the team's guidelines*, so that the system is as simple, as well-tested, and as agile as possible. (See Part VI.)

- *To implement only what is necessary*, to keep the project as simple and as valuable as possible for the customer. (See Part VI.)

- *To communicate constantly with the customer*, to understand his concerns and to help him to make accurate scheduling decisions. (See "Business Practice 1: Add a Customer to the Team" in Part II.)

Supplementary Roles

XP discusses two other roles. They might not be present in a formal capacity on every team.

The Tracker

The tracker keeps track of the schedule. XP tracks a few metrics. The most important is team velocity, which is the ratio of ideal time estimated for tasks to the actual time spent implementing them. Other important data may include any changes in velocity, the amount of overtime worked, and the ratio of passing tests to failing tests.

All of these numbers measure progress and the rate of progress. They help determine if the project is on schedule for the iteration. They can signal behavioral changes that may affect the schedule. Looking at the numbers alone rarely gives the whole picture; anomalies should be brought before the whole team for analysis during the stand-up meeting (see "The Iteration" in Part III.)

To measure velocity within the iteration, every day or two, the tracker asks each developer how many tasks she has completed. This is best done in person, as informally and comfortably as possible. Honesty is vital on the part of developers, and the tracker should be nonjudgmental. This may be a manager or a trusted developer. Regularly tracking progress helps the team adjust to its ebb and flow of work.

The Coach

Some XP projects have a coach who guides and mentors the team. This can be helpful when adopting XP. His position is one of respect—he leads by example.

XP can be difficult to apply consistently. Though many of its practices are common sense, the skills they require take time to develop. There are also occasional obstacles and subtleties that require the wisdom of a master. The coach's main virtue is his experience.

The coach guides his team to understand XP and software development. Sometimes he teaches directly. Sometimes he rolls up his sleeves and teaches by doing. He may suggest changes in how a practice is implemented, offer ideas to solve a thorny technical problem, or serve as an intermediary between the team and other management.

PART VI

Coding, XP Style

*XP wants systems that are well positioned
for current, actual change.*

—Kent Beck[*]

XP's goals are simple. Software should be well-tested and expressive. It should have no unnecessary features. Developers should be confident in their ability to meet future needs. Customers should receive the software they really need. XP can make it easier to meet these goals, but really trusting that they're achievable is hard.

XP developers use several catchphrases to remind themselves of the goal of flexibility through simplicity. These sayings are *Do the Simplest Thing that Could Possibly Work*, *You Aren't Gonna Need It*, and *Once and Only Once*. Understanding and applying these ideas will help you to produce code that can be changed to meet future needs.

Do the Simplest Thing That Could Possibly Work

The phrase "Do the Simplest Thing that Could Possibly Work" is a reminder to balance functionality with simplicity. Ideally, code is designed and implemented as simply as possible while passing all tests. Comprehensive tests anchor

---

[*] *http://c2.com/ppr/wiki/WikiPagesAboutRefactoring/OaooBalancesYagni.html*

the code to its necessary behavior. Merciless refactoring revises the code into its simplest possible representation.

Diligently practicing simplicity invests developer time in the customer's current need, where it counts the most. Do what you need to do. Solve the current problem. Implement it simply. Make it work, then clean it up. Leave the whole system as simple as possible.

XP purposefully leaves "simplest" vague. It's up to you to decide what is appropriate in each situation. Maybe using a library or reusing code elsewhere in the system is the simplest thing. The simplest thing may be refactoring another piece of code into a reusable class to use for the current task. Simplicity usually means not building in unnecessary flexibility; don't add bells and whistles you don't need.

"Simple" is different from "quickest to write" and very different from "the first idea that comes to mind." Discovering the simplest possible solution is difficult. It's okay to settle for simple enough, especially since you will refactor later. Simplify further when you come up with a better idea.

Simple code is easier to write after you break the habit of guessing ahead at future needs. Follow the story and task cards. Avoid the temptation to ask "what if?" If the requirements are unclear or if there are gaps in the stories, ask the customer for clarification. Simple code is easier to understand. A method of five lines is likely clearer than a method of fifty or a hundred lines. Simple code is easier to test—and test-driven development produces simpler code. Simpler code is easier to improve.

Practicing test-driven development is an excellent way to achieve simplicity of implementation. Every line of code must exist to pass a test. Given comprehensive test coverage, any code that can be deleted without causing a test to fail should be deleted. Practiced with extreme discipline, this forces simplicity in the small. Test in small steps, one piece of a feature at a time. Add the simplest code that could possibly pass the current test. Simplify the code by refactoring.

Consider a simulated candy machine. If the machine only holds one item, that item can be hardcoded in the get_items method. Add the flexibility to contain more items only when a failing test prompts you to do so. Add a test that checks for more items only when a task card prompts you to do so. You will find that your code can be far simpler than you thought possible.

After the current test passes, look for refactoring opportunities. Can the code you just wrote be refactored? Was it simpler to copy and paste code than to write a more generalized function? Did you duplicate code elsewhere? When the tests all pass, you have the opportunity to improve the design in the large. Make the most of it.

XP practices continual design, letting you make design decisions at any time. With every new story, you'll see the design more clearly. With every implemented task, you'll have more fuel for refactoring.

Actively seeking simplicity can feel counterintuitive. Good developers often want to guard against future cases. Resist that temptation! XP produces systems that can be changed easily not by being complex enough to handle every possibility, but by being simple enough to be changed. Hone your instincts to write code that can grow to meet needs as they become known.

You Aren't Gonna Need It

The phrase "You Aren't Gonna Need It" is a reminder to do today's work today and tomorrow's work tomorrow. It's tempting to work on future requirements, but it is risky to invest in features that *may* be necessary at the expense of features that *are* necessary now. Spending time and resources on one task leaves less time and fewer resources for other tasks. Implement only the features you need when you need them.

The temptation to build in extra flexibility comes from two motivations. The first is fear. Many software projects are brittle and inflexible. Dragons lurk in dusty, dark corners. A simple bugfix may have repercussions throughout the codebase. Practicing XP with discipline can conquer this fear. Your tests will allow you to make changes with confidence. Refactoring will keep your code flexible. Doing the simplest thing that could possibly work will produce understandable and changeable code.

The second motivation is the desire to work on "interesting bits." Exploring the latest and greatest new library or fine-tuning a complicated new algorithm can be exciting. However, writing code for an unrequested and unscheduled feature undermines the customer's business authority just as the customer mentally halving your estimates undermines your judgment.

Anticipating future needs is gambling. If the customer someday actually requests an unrequested feature, will it take the same shape as when you first thought of it? Will the customer even ever ask for the feature? The customer's business may change unexpectedly and a feature you thought would be vitally important may be rendered completely unnecessary. You may occasionally guess correctly, but balance the cost of waiting against the risk of predicting the future.

Further, unused features complicate the code with baggage that meets no immediate needs. At best, unused code will be deleted unceremoniously. More likely, it will remain entrenched and will be worked around. Every new feature adds complexity to the code. It's more code to test, more to refactor, and more to maintain.

Trust the customer to identify necessary features when they're needed. Solve today's problems today. Invest in testing, coding, and refactoring features that pay off now. Simple, well-factored code leaves your options open in the future. Add features when you need them, refactoring them into the design as if they'd always been there.

Once and Only Once

The phrase "Once and Only Once" is a reminder of a goal of refactoring. Every piece of knowledge within the system should be represented in a single, well-known place. Eliminate repetition.

The Pragmatic Programmer, by Andrew Hunt and David Thomas (Addison-Wesley), suggests a slightly different rule: *Don't Repeat Yourself* (DRY). The difference is subtle. Once and Only Once suggests eliminating duplication through refactoring. It applies to code and design concepts. The DRY principle goes further. It applies to code and design but also other project artifacts. For example, if you find yourself performing the same steps while integrating, automate them. Both principles apply; solve a problem once and for all.

Duplication and repetition are warning signs. Any time knowledge is duplicated, it's possible for the versions to fall out of sync, as is often the case with code and comments. Repeated code is an obvious opportunity for refactoring—it can signify that your abstractions should be made more powerful or that your code can be generalized.

Repetition and duplication produce inertia. It takes longer to make a change that requires touching several different pieces of code. It is more difficult to make a change if the responsibilities are scattered throughout the code. You'll have to rely on your memory. Comprehensive tests may not help: if every duplicate section has its own tests, you can't make a change and rely on test failures to identify everything you need to update.

Once and Only Once complements You Aren't Gonna Need It. The latter recommends against adding complexity. The former advises finding and removing complexity. It is difficult to anticipate all complexity and duplication in advance, so refactor it away when you find it.

Knowing when to reduce duplication can be tricky. The first time you write some code, leave it as simple as possible. The second time you write similar code, refactor just enough to remove the duplication. By the third time, you'll probably know enough to generalize the code to most cases you will encounter.

Once and Only Once applies to more than code. Automate every process that's worth automating. If you find yourself performing a task many times, script it. This can be anything from generating header files to logging integration failures. The principle also applies to documentation and other written artifacts. The test suites and the code itself are the canonical representation of the business knowledge of the project. The tests identify what the code should do. The code describes how it is done. Any further documentation should complement—not duplicate—this knowledge, or risk becoming useless, out-of-date baggage.

XP values code that is easily changed and easily maintained. Rigorous testing and simplicity produce small, loosely coupled units. Refactoring adds cohesion. Though the structure of the code changes over time, gradual adjustments help the project converge on its optimal design. Eliminating duplication and repetition speeds this process.

PART VII

Adopting XP

XP works because its practices complement each other. It's a whole package. Of course, few projects have the luxury of starting from scratch with a new development process. Few developers are talented and courageous enough to be perfectly productive in new circumstances. Few organizations are flexible enough to listen to all of the weird ideas that just might work, let alone to try the best ones.

Furthermore, XP doesn't fit every situation completely. You may not be able to convince your manager to try pair programming. You may not be able to find a customer to speak with a single voice. You might need to improve your teamwork before you can think about practicing collective code ownership.

Many projects adopt XP in stages. Introducing XP gradually requires care and discipline. Certain practices are risky without the support of others. Some organizations need to see practical results before committing more fully. It's important to weigh the strengths and weaknesses of XP and your team before jumping in with both feet.

Though some practices obviously precede others, there are many possible paths toward full XP adoption. This chapter describes one way to adopt XP. It presumes you're a developer on an existing project. You don't necessarily need management approval to start, though it may give you the political capital necessary to adopt further practices that do need management support.

Adopting XP means doing what makes the most sense for your team. The best approach is to adopt the most important practice first. Identify your biggest and most pressing need. Solve it. Repeat with the next biggest need.

Before You Start

Before you start adopting XP, you must have a few things already in place. First, you need a team of developers. You should all get along and you should all have some practical experience. You don't need a team of experts, though having one or two gurus can help.

You need a good source control system. You must be able to work on the system without getting in the way of each other. There must be one single place that holds the most complete, most recent version of the code. It's very handy to be able to merge and revert changes if necessary. This will save you time.

You must have a customer, though her role can be informal for now. She must have a problem for you to solve. Your goal must be to solve her problem.

As a team of developers, you must be willing to try XP. It's okay to be skeptical; you can adopt the first few principles and see if and how they improve your work. Adopting XP by yourself in a big team is likely to cause more friction than positive results. Of course, having one developer who refuses to try XP is also difficult. It's more productive to find a compromise than to work around him.

The first step to adopting XP is to build a healthy team.

Eliminating Fear and Working Together

XP can succeed only when developers want to produce good software as a team. You must be able to trust each other's work. It's easier to do the right thing if all of your coworkers are doing the same. Trust and honesty will dispel many fears that would otherwise slow or sink the project.

Developing coding standards (see "Coding Practice 3: Develop Coding Standards" in Part II) can really bring your developers together. A healthy team can produce a small and useful set of community standards for all new code, including refactorings. These standards are idioms and phrases, a common vocabulary for developers to communicate through working code. Well-defined standards make it much easier to adopt the other XP coding practices.

Adopt a common vocabulary (see "Coding Practice 4: Develop a Common Vocabulary" in Part II) with the coding standards. XP relies heavily on communication. Just as design patterns help communicate designs and design strategies through metaphor, common names and ideas help communicate features and stories. Make that as easy as possible as soon as possible.

Both your coding standards and your common vocabulary will evolve with time. Start small, but start soon. Bring everyone on board early, agree on a few ground rules, and let the whole team decide on changes as necessary.

Start coding and designing simply (see "Coding Practice 1: Code and Design Simply" in Part II). It will take time to break the habit of coding unnecessary flexibility. Start removing unnecessary code soon. Develop confidence in your abilities to meet future needs by adapting simple code. Your next goal will be to demonstrate that your simple code and simple design actually does what it needs to do.

Starting Feedback

As your team continues to improve, start gathering feedback. This will allow you to see change occurring and to adapt to it. If you're fortunate enough to have a customer right now, great! Getting her feedback will help guide your development. If not, you can still learn from the feedback loops within the coding process.

The most important question right now is "Does the code work?" The only way to know is to test it (see "Developer Practice 1: Adopt Test-Driven Development" in Part II). Test-driven development will give you immediate confidence that the current code acts as it should and long-term assurance that new bugs and regressions can be fixed quickly. You must trust each other to write new tests, to run existing tests, and to fix broken tests.

It's much easier to start testing from the beginning, but few projects have that luxury. Halting new development to add tests retroactively is unpleasant and time consuming. Instead, adopt test-driven development for all new features, including bugfixes.

Writing a test for a bug before you fix it has several benefits. First, it defers the cost of retroactive testing until it's needed. Noticing the bug tells you the code is wrong. Capture that knowledge in a test! Second, it adds tests where they're most needed. Third, it prevents the bug from reoccurring. (Too often bugs are fixed and subsequently unfixed several times.) The buggiest—likely ugliest—sections of your code will benefit from ever-improving test coverage.

Though unit testing is easier to start, don't skimp on acceptance tests. They can be more difficult to write without a real customer, but their feedback is valuable to monitor user-level changes. As with unit tests, start adding acceptance tests for new features and bugfixes.

Start adopting the planning game now (see "Business Practice 2: Play the Planning Game" in Part II). It can be difficult to write story cards without an actual customer to represent business concerns; however, you can still break feature requests into tasks and estimate them now. This will help you refine your estimating skills and reinforce your burgeoning habit of doing the simplest thing that could possibly work (see "Do the Simplest Thing That Could Possibly Work" in Part VI). It will also help you to work in smaller pieces.

With good tests and small tasks, you can practice continual integration (see "Developer Practice 4: Integrate Continually" in Part II). The smaller the task, the easier it is to merge changes into your code repository. The better the tests, the faster you can see if your changes broke anything. Every new feature added to the system solidifies its design a little more. Working in small tasks and integrating them often rapidly spreads changes through the system.

All of these practices pave the way for collective code ownership (see "Developer Practice 3: Adopt Collective Code Ownership" in Part II). An effective test suite gives you the confidence to make bigger changes. Small tasks help you avoid conflicts that come from working on the same sections of code. Simple designs and coding standards help you to read and comprehend other pieces of code.

Refactoring (see "Coding Practice 2: Refactor Mercilessly" in Part II) comes next. You already have the goal of simplicity and the guidelines of coding standards to drive the refactoring. You have tests to preserve the external behavior of the code. Look for ways to improve the code, and then make those changes! It's tempting to make big, sweeping changes, but remember to tidy in small steps. Refactoring can be risky without comprehensive tests, but it's possible. Before you clean up under-tested code, add an acceptance test or two for safety.

Your productivity should be improving with feedback from test-driven development, refactoring, and their supporting practices. If you're new to this style of work, you'll be a little slower at first. Keep at it. Soon, the light bulb will go on in your head and you'll proceed with confidence and agility.

This is a good time to assess yourselves as a team. What are you learning? If you're struggling, find out why. Are you not working together closely enough? Are some developers not testing enough? Do you just need more time to figure things out? Talk it over, make a plan, and carry it out. If you're producing better software—and you probably are—it will be easier to adopt further XP practices, especially those that require business support.

Including Managers and Customers

Your next goal is to get regular, direct customer involvement. This meets the XP values of honesty and communication. If you can include the customer from the start, great! If not, you can still improve your development process. The real gains will come when you do add a customer to your team (see "Business Practice 1: Add a Customer to the Team" in Part II).

There's no substitute for an actual customer, although some teams use a customer proxy out of necessity. Your manager might represent a customer, or you might find a customer representative who can sit with your project regularly. Without a real customer, it can be difficult to juggle developer and business concerns. However you proceed, the customer *must* keep business interests in mind and *must* have the final authority on business matters.

Adding a customer helps everyone adjust to the idea of divided roles and responsibilities (see Part V). The earlier you can do this, the better. Blurring business and technical responsibilities, especially story scheduling, can undermine the customer's investment. It's better to be explicit about who makes which decisions.

With a customer in place, the planning game is more effective. Internally, the team can write its own stories and plan its own iterations within a larger milestone schedule, but the point of XP is to adjust to the customer's needs as quickly and flexibly as possible. These needs are communicated through the planning game.

With a customer in place, regular releases are also possible (see "Business Practice 3: Release Regularly" in Part II). You can play the planning game in full. Code is well-tested and is integrated regularly. You can start working in iterations, planning small, regular migrations. They're less painful that way.

At this point, you can demonstrate to the customer and other business interests your ability to adapt to change. Let the customer drive the schedule. You're flexible enough now to meet future needs as they arise.

Sane iteration schedules and well-tested code will let you work at a sustainable pace (see "Business Practice 4: Work at a Sustainable Pace" in Part II). It's possible to adopt this practice earlier as code quality improves. The planning game makes it workable. Yesterday, you did as much work as you could. You scheduled the same amount of work for today. There's sufficient time today for today's work. Tomorrow's work will be there tomorrow.

The final practice remaining is pair programming (see "Developer Practice 2: Practice Pair Programming" in Part II). It's easier to introduce if you have appropriate facilities, which may require your manager to approve moving away from cubicles into a bullpen (see "The Bullpen" in Part IV). Ideally, you can introduce this earlier—it's a great way to reinforce trust and teamwork.

Pair programming can be scary, though. Many projects assume that the amount of code produced corresponds directly with productivity. Pairing two developers on one feature would seem to halve the team's velocity. Code production is a poor metric, though—practices like coding simply and refactoring often reduce the amount of code in a system. Besides, by pairing you can often produce better code with less debugging time. You may have to back up this argument with actual proof of your declining bug counts and improving test counts, however.

Regardless of perception, adopting pair programming is vital to the long-term health of the project. The sooner you can pair for all production code, the healthier your code will be. Developers of extraordinary discipline may write elegant, well-tested code all the time. The rest of us sometimes need positive peer pressure and reinforcement.

Now That You're Extreme

With all 12 practices in place, you're reaping the full rewards of XP. New code is easier to write. New features are easier to add. Bug counts are down, and the few bugs that are introduced are easier to fix. Your customer is happy and you're finding new enjoyment in your work.

That's not the end of the story, though.

No development process can fully protect you from mistakes. The best it can do is to give you tools to prevent, identify, and adapt to crises. Of course, the same tools may help or hinder you from taking advantage of new opportunities. Your own experience and skills—honed and guided by a good process—are the best tools in your toolbox.

The real magic of XP comes when you take control of it. Your team has its own quirks and characteristics. Some are positive and some are negative. Tweak XP to your advantage. Maybe moving the last day of an iteration to Wednesday morning will give you time to react to immediate feedback before the weekend. Maybe adding a priority field to story cards will help the customer keep long-term milestones in mind. Always look for the next problem to solve.

Neither you nor your customers have to fear change anymore. Experiment. Find your biggest obstacle, solve it, and look for the next obstacle. Make little adjustments. Listen for feedback. You'll be able to adapt to any situation.

PART VIII

Further Resources

XP is an active and evolving discipline. It's under continual refinement, moving into new areas and being understood more fully. Keeping abreast of the latest knowledge can help you introduce XP in new situations. Furthermore, any team without a coach (see "The Coach" in Part V) may run into areas of confusion where a little advice can be golden.

XP Resources

These resources are starting points to explore XP further. The best way to understand it is to do it. The second best way is to learn from people who are doing it successfully.

- Ward Cunningham's Wiki at *http://c2.com/cgi/wiki* is the best place to explore XP as it evolves. It's populated by thoughtful, intelligent people with tremendous wisdom. If you've never used a Wiki before, lurk for a while. The community standards and evolutionary process resemble XP in many important ways.

- Ron Jeffries' *http://www.xprogramming.com/* has several interesting resources, including the online XP Magazine (*http://www.xprogramming.com/xpmag/index.htm*).

- Don Wells' *http://www.extremeprogramming.org/* features a gentle introduction to XP. The lessons learned by XP teams (*http://www.extremeprogramming.org/lessons.html*) are of particular interest.

- The JUnit home page (*http://junit.org/*) hosts the canonical unit-testing framework for Java, originally written by Kent Beck and Erich Gamma, and ported to several other languages. (See *http://www.xprogramming.com/software.htm* for these other frameworks.) The JUnit site also has links to several useful testing articles.

- Ward Cunningham has created another testing framework called FIT, which can be found at *http://fit.c2.com/*. FIT allows data-driven testing and makes tests very easy to write, especially for customers.

- The Extreme Programming mailing list (*http://groups.yahoo.com/group/extremeprogramming/*) is a high-quality mailing list devoted to discussing XP issues and practices. It's frequented by people who are applying XP successfully in many different projects.

- The Agile Alliance (*http://www.agilealliance.org/*) is a lightweight organization dedicated to promoting and helping companies adopt agile development methods. See the Agile Manifesto (*http://www.agilemanifesto.org/*) for information about their goals. XP is one of several recognized Agile processes.

- Martin Fowler maintains *http://www.refactoring.com/*, which is devoted to his book, *Refactoring: Improving the Design of Existing Code* (Addison-Wesley). The list of refactoring tools at *http://www.refactoring.com/tools.html* is particularly useful.

- The refactoring mailing list (*http://groups.yahoo.com/group/refactoring*) is another good refactoring resource.

- A study performed at the University of Utah sought to prove that pair programming produced software products of better quality in less time with happier, more confident programmers. The researchers, Laurie Williams and Robert R. Kessler, published their results in a study entitled "Strengthening the Case for Pair Programming" (*http://www.cs.utah.edu/~lwilliam/Papers/ieeeSoftware.PDF*).

- A University of Michigan School of Information study on facilities and programmer productivity found that war rooms (see "The Bullpen" in Part IV) had dramatic benefits. Further, they found that programmers preferred working together after their experiences (see *http://www. si.umich.edu/features/0101-warrooms.htm*).

Index

We'd like to hear your suggestions for improving our indexes. Send email to
index@oreilly.com.

Need in-depth answers fast?

O'REILLY NETWORK
Safari® Bookshelf.

Access over 2,000 of the newest and best technology books online

Safari Bookshelf is the premier electronic reference library for IT professionals and programmers—a must-have when you need to pinpoint exact answers in an instant.

Access over 2,000 of the top technical reference books by twelve leading publishers including O'Reilly, Addison-Wesley, Peachpit Press, Prentice Hall, and Microsoft Press. Safari provides the technical references and code samples you need to develop quality, timely solutions.

Try it today with a FREE TRIAL
Visit *www.oreilly.com/safari/max*

For groups of five or more, set up a free, 30-day corporate trial
Contact: *corporate@oreilly.com*

Keep in touch with O'Reilly

1. Download examples from our books

To find example files for a book, go to:
www.oreilly.com/catalog

select the book, and follow the "Examples" link.

2. Register your O'Reilly books

Register your book at *register.oreilly.com*

Why register your books? Once you've registered your O'Reilly books you can:

- Win O'Reilly books, T-shirts or discount coupons in our monthly drawing.
- Get special offers available only to registered O'Reilly customers.
- Get catalogs announcing new books (US and UK only).
- Get email notification of new editions of the O'Reilly books you own.

3. Join our email lists

Sign up to get topic-specific email announcements of new books and conferences, special offers, and O'Reilly Network technology newsletters at:
elists.oreilly.com

It's easy to customize your free elists subscription so you'll get exactly the O'Reilly news you want.

4. Get the latest news, tips, and tools
www.oreilly.com

- "Top 100 Sites on the Web"—PC Magazine
- CIO Magazine's Web Business 50 Awards

Our web site contains a library of comprehensive product information (including book excerpts and tables of contents), downloadable software, background articles, interviews with technology leaders, links to relevant sites, book cover art, and more.

5. Work for O'Reilly

Check out our web site for current employment opportunities:
jobs.oreilly.com

6. Contact us

O'Reilly & Associates
1005 Gravenstein Hwy North
Sebastopol, CA 95472 USA

TEL: 707-827-7000 or 800-998-9938
(6am to 5pm PST)

FAX: 707-829-0104

order@oreilly.com
For answers to problems regarding your order or our products.
To place a book order online, visit:
www.oreilly.com/order_new

catalog@oreilly.com
To request a copy of our latest catalog.

booktech@oreilly.com
For book content technical questions or corrections.

corporate@oreilly.com
For educational, library, government, and corporate sales.

proposals@oreilly.com
To submit new book proposals to our editors and product managers.

international@oreilly.com
For information about our international distributors or translation queries. For a list of our distributors outside of North America check out:
international.oreilly.com/distributors.html

adoption@oreilly.com
For information about academic use of O'Reilly books, visit:
academic.oreilly.com

O'REILLY®

Our books are available at most retail and online bookstores.
To order direct: 1-800-998-9938 • *order@oreilly.com* • *www.oreilly.com*
Online editions of most O'Reilly titles are available at *safari.oreilly.com*